Scotland's Enterprise Deficit

About the authors

Professor Sir Donald MacKay
is chairman of Grampian Holdings and the Edinburgh Business School. A former chairman of Scottish Enterprise (1993-97) he has had a distinguished academic career, as Professor of Political Economy at Aberdeen University and Professor of Economics at Heriot Watt University.
He is a trustee of The Policy Institute.

Dr James Cuthbert
A former lecturer in statistics at Glasgow University, Dr Cuthbert joined the Civil Service as a statistician in 1974, working mainly in the Scottish Office, but also, for two years, in the Treasury. Since retiring as Scottish Office chief statistician in 1997, he has, inter alia, pursued research projects in the theory of international purchasing power comparisons and on topics in the Scottish Office.

Margaret Cuthbert
is an economist. Starting work in ICI, she has subsequently lectured in Glasgow and Heriot Watt Universities, but has spent most of her career working as an economics consultant. Her main interests are enterprise and the knowledge economy.

Gerry Dowds
is Director of the Forum of Private Business (Scotland) and a main board director of the Forum of Private Business. He joined FPB in 1979 and has been active in marketing and advocacy functions north and south of the border. Having spent 16 years in Chester, he returned to Stirling in April 1999 to re-launch FPB in Scotland.

Alastair Balfour
is a businessman, private investor and writer. A journalist to trade, he co-founded and was managing director of the Insider business publishing group before its sale in 1999. He is now a private investor in, and director of, a number of Scottish companies. For 13 years he has written a weekly business column, primarily about the owner-managed business sector.
He is co-author of the forthcoming Dorling Kindersley book "Working from Home".

Professor Sir Donald MacKay

Scotland's Enterprise Deficit
What is it
What can be done

Additional contributions from
Jim and Margaret Cuthbert
Gerry Dowds
Alastair Balfour

Acknowledgements
PricewaterhouseCoopers

The Policy Institute is very grateful to PricewaterhouseCoopers for its financial support towards the publication of Professor MacKay's paper. An earlier version was prepared as a confidential report for the Royal Bank of Scotland and we are grateful to RBS for its permission to extend and update the analysis. Neither party is to blame for any errors of omission or commission, which remain the sole responsibility of the author, while the views expressed by Professor MacKay and the other authors (who write in a personal capacity) are their own.

About the Policy Institute

Who we are, what we seek to do

The Policy Institute is dedicated to the promotion of liberal market values and solutions.
Its aim is to investigate, research and promote social and economic policies which will encourage the development of Scotland as a prosperous market economy within the United Kingdom.
The Institute has been established as a research and educational charitable trust. It is independent of all political parties and political organisations. It has an ambitious programme of publications, meetings and seminars.
It is financed by voluntary donations from the public and by corporate donation and support. It is governed by a group of independent managing trustees drawn from different walks of Scottish life. A foundation supported by the Barclay brothers has provided initial funding, and they have generously pledged to match funding from other sources up to a certain limit.
The Institute will publish, to the highest professional and editorial standards, pamphlets and monographs designed to encourage debate on a wide range of topics, and to offer original and radical solutions. It also intends to publish commentary on the work of the Scottish Executive and Parliament.

How you can help

The Policy Institute is a registered charity and relies entirely on voluntary donations and private subscription and support. You can help in a number of ways, first, by making a donation to the work of the Institute, second by agreeing to sponsor a specific topic for publication and discussion, and third by agreeing to help fund the Institute's work by covenanted support.

The Institute's immediate task is to prepare and present an initial range of publications and for these to be published and distributed requires financial support, both individual and corporate.

Contents

A section of colour charts appears between pages 24 and 25

Introduction

A damning policy failure

Eight years after Scottish Enterprise embarked on an ambitious campaign to close the gap in business formation rates between Scotland and the rest of the UK, Scotland continues to lag. Moreover, its business start-up rate is now falling, not rising. This is Scotland's enterprise deficit. Why has this policy failed? And what should now be done?

A low business start-up rate remains one of the most persistent and worrying features of Scotland's economy. Scots, relative to their counterparts in the rest of the UK, seem unwilling, or unable, to launch new businesses, to respond entrepreneurially, to "give it a go". Why should this be? What is the nature and extent of this relatively low business formation rate? Why does it persist? And what can be done to raise the rate of new business start-ups?

These are among the most pressing questions facing policymakers. A high business birth rate is central to Scotland's future as a vibrant and successful economy. Study after study has underlined the link between high levels of business start-up and economic growth, and the role of new business as a driver of employment, innovation, enterprise and economic performance. Yet despite the earnest endeavours of Scottish Enterprise, not only is Scotland continuing to lag the rest of the UK in new business formation, but the rate of business start-up in Scotland is now in absolute decline (**see chart 1**).

This enterprise deficit is, as we examine here, partly the result of cultural factors. It is also, one senses, part of a wider and more problematic under-appreciation of the importance of small businesses in the wider economy.

Policy-making underplays the needs and concerns of small firms. The "business voice" is too readily assumed to be catered for by the big battalions of the Confederation of British Industry and establishment tycoons so assiduously courted by government and co-opted into the government process itself or one of its quasi-autonomous agencies. Yet taking the broad definition of small business – firms employing up to 99 people - the figures are startling. There are 3.7 million in total in Britain. They account for 99 per cent of the total business population, 44 per cent of total turnover and 51 per cent of the total employed in business.

Why are their concerns not more widely understood? The statistics give us a clue. There may be 3.7 million businesses, but just 1.6 million of these are registered for VAT. This suggests more than half of all small firms go unrecorded in many business monitoring statistics and opinion surveys because they are "under the radar" for VAT and thus do not formally exist when it comes to policy-making and drafting of legislation that critically affects business.

This point is of particular relevance in Scotland. According to latest DTI statistics, there were 233,400 small and medium sized companies in Scotland at the start of 1999. Together they employed 1.5 million, or just over 60 per cent of all employed in business. This SME employment share compares with 58 per cent in the South East of England, 54 per cent across England as a whole, and 42.5 per cent in the London area. SMEs are therefore a more, not less, important part of the business constituency in Scotland and thus deserve to rank higher in policy thinking and determination.

It is thus appropriate that the first publication of the Policy Institute is devoted to the question of the enterprise deficit. We are fortunate in being able to draw upon an outstanding analysis by Professor Sir Donald MacKay, chairman of Grampian plc and a former chairman of Scottish Enterprise. Not only does his paper The

Business Birth Rate: Scotland's Achilles Heel provide a wealth of data on this issue in clear and authoritative form, but it also lays out key implications for policy.

The Institute is further indebted to other prominent writers and commentators. The economists Jim and Margaret Cuthbert, and Gerry Dowds of the Forum of Private Business, discuss the issue of non-domestic rates reform. The writer and businessman Alastair Balfour provides an eloquent plea on business regulation. The Institute has supplemented these contributions with panels and boxes of key facts and statistics for students and business users.

The two issues of rates and regulation emerge as recurrent concerns among small companies. The size of the rates burden is substantial. Through the non-domestic, or business rate, which falls due before even a penny of revenue is generated or profit made, Scotland's businesses pay up a total of £1.3 billion a year, equivalent to almost one third of all local authority non-government grant income. It is here that the policy bias against small business is at its most acute. Too often businesses are cast as negatives in the community, or as costs, or passive absorbers of benefits. In fact, they enjoy very little in the way of representation for the £1.3 billion they provide. And they receive very little by way of direct, specific services such as refuse collection, which they have to finance themselves. There is too little recognition of the role small firms play in sustaining a community, contributing to its vibrancy and diversity, providing employment and sustaining specific and particular services validated every day by the market. Yes, communities create businesses, and, we would add, *vice versa*.

Searching for the policy impact

This is by no means the first study in Scotland on business start-up. Nor does it claim to be the most comprehensive. But its appearance now is timely for two reasons. The first is the recent admitted failure of Scottish Enterprise, a £500 million a year taxpayer funded public agency, to narrow the gap between Scotland and the rest of the UK in new business formation – the goal it expressly set itself eight years ago. Indeed, not only has the gap remained as wide as ever, with Scotland achieving just 83 per cent of the UK rate of new business formation. The rate of new business start-ups is also falling in absolute terms. In 1999 business start-ups fell 16 per cent on the previous year, a rate of decline that has continued into the first half of 2000. **(see charts 1 and 2)**

What is particularly striking is that this gap has persisted despite a markedly benign economic backdrop. This begs the question that if policy fails so signally in periods of strong macro-economic performance, when would it ever succeed? The UK economy has enjoyed the longest unbroken period of sustained growth since the war. The period has also seen the commitment of millions of pounds by Scottish Enterprise in local enterprise centres, "strategic thrusts", "enterprise learning experi-

ences", "focused support" and a series of detailed studies into the encouragement of enterprise and public attitudes towards entrepreneurship. This work has been well resourced. In its marketing and communications it has lacked for nothing. Indeed, one sometimes feels with Scottish Enterprise that marketing is supreme, that it has become the endgame, rather than the underlying work or the project it is seeking to promote.

Given this notably benign economic backdrop in the period 1992-2000, it is difficult to discern what specific difference the agency may or may not have made to new business start-up **(see chart 3)**. Indeed, on the same premise that Scottish Enterprise attributed the recent slowdown in business start-ups to general economic conditions[1], so it should also recognise the contribution made by benign economic conditions to the improvement in business formation rates between 1992 and 1997. Until there is a fully independent assessment of the impact of the work of Scottish

[1] See Network News release December 13, Scottish Enterprise: "Our own recent review of the decline in the New Business Statistic, carried out with the Scottish Executive, suggested that the principle (sic) causes of this reduction have been economic in character..."

Enterprise in this field, the question persists: why has there been a failure to demonstrate non cyclical, structural improvements in business formation rates? What really has changed?

Arguably most depressing of all is that Scottish Enterprise seems no nearer to a grasp of what is going wrong and what it should be doing than in 1993 when the Business Start-up Strategy was launched. It has recently turned to the Fraser of Allander Institute to conduct a review "and seek to draw out the key lessons to be learned in terms of the future direction of policy for the Scottish Enterprise Network."[2]

An emperor with no clothes

Seldom can there have been such a damning policy shortfall. This brings us to the second reason for this Policy Institute pamphlet now. For seldom can a policy failure of this expense and magnitude have tiptoed by with barely a murmur from the Scottish parliament and the political establishment in Scotland. Few dare to suggest that on

the question of business start-up and the promotion of entrepreneurialism, we have in Scotland an enterprise emperor with no clothes.

The issue of business start-up is complex – from measuring the problem to creating that vital supportive culture. For example, most business start-ups are not captured in the official statistics because these only capture companies that have registered for VAT. Most commentators breezily assume that firms below the VAT line are simply not significant in the big macro picture. But many successful businesses do start with the determination of one or two individuals and a notebook and calculator on the kitchen table. And while many little businesses may not employ more than a handful, they are, as we have seen, users and generators of other business services in their local areas and thus have a significant indirect impact on employment overall.

Even in setting targets, Scottish Enterprise may have made a cardinal error. The initial target in 1993 was to

[2] See Network News, December 13 2000, Scottish Enterprise.

close the gap with the rest of the UK in terms of the annual number of new business created. Simply by closing the gap, the strategy suggested, would result in 25,000 additional businesses and at least 50,000 new jobs.

The South East pull-away

But as Professor MacKay's paper makes powerfully clear, the UK figures are lifted significantly by London and the South East where, because of the explosion in global financial services, business formation is by far the highest in the country. For example, the number of registered businesses per 10,000 population is highest in London at 351. The comparable figure for Scotland is 229. And VAT registrations as a proportion of the business stock in Great Britain outside London and the South East is significantly lower than that for GB as a whole[3]. Among the key findings of Professor MacKay's research is that business density (measured by the number of VAT registered businesses per 10,000 population) not only remains below the average for Great Britain (16.4 per cent below the GB average in 1999 against 16.3 per cent in 1980) but also that the gap between Scotland and London and the south east has widened significantly over the period.

Yet this finding can hardly have come as a surprise to Scottish Enterprise. Its own research flashed up a warning signal at the outset of the Business Start-up scheme in 1992 that "to narrow the gap Scotland has to achieve a company birth rate (measured as a percentage of the stock) significantly above that of southern England."[4] But for Scotland's aspirant entrepreneurs to be set a target for closing the start-up rate with the rest of the UK including London and the South East was akin to setting them off on a manic chase after an ever accelerating electric hare. It assumed high unemployment areas like East Ayrshire could perform at least as well as a distinctly non-cohort group that contained the City of London. As the decade wore on and the economic performance of London and the South East streaked

[3]For details, see Professor MacKay's paper and related charts

[4]*Scotland's Business Birth Rate*, Scottish Enterprise, 1992, p.5

11

ahead, that benchmark target became ever more unrealistic. Result: failure, frustration and demoralisation.

Professor MacKay's paper is important in another aspect, arguing that the relatively lower rate of business start-up in Scotland cannot be attributed to faults in the provision of finance. This question needed to be analysed in some detail. Not only is it most commonly cited as a problem by people thinking of starting a business (around 50 per cent compared with less than 20 per cent cited for all other potential problems), but also because the belief in some systemic or inherent flaw in the banking system remains one of the potent myths on the Left. While there is often justifiable criticism of some banks in their understanding of changing business needs and their methods of service delivery [5] the absence of available loan finance is not, per se, the chief problem.

Attitudes to enterprise

One recurring concern has been an unduly negative attitude in Scotland towards entrepreneurs. The same culture that spawned so many breakthroughs in the industrial revolution, that created a breed of swashbuckling émigré titans of industry and finance throughout the English speaking world, seemed by the early 1980s to have all but vanished in the country's leading educational establishment and political institutions. With some distinguished exceptions, many of Scotland's outstanding entrepreneurs have left the country for bigger opportunities or sold out to larger businesses. Others have become fossilised on the boards of museum-piece investment trusts. This has had the effect of leaving Scotland largely in the hands of a socialistic rump that had turned in on itself, or retreated into a Scandinavian enclave of cradle to grave welfare provision. It is one characterised by a constant grumbling about resources, a relentless hectoring pursuit of political correctness agendas, the treatment of business as little more than a milch cow, and a cramping, crushing timidity of purpose

[5] See *Private Business and their banks, 2000*. Forum of Private Business, November 2000. This heavily criticised the Clydesdale and Bank of Scotland in particular for poor service delivery to small business customers, while other banks fared much better in survey responses.

and vision. "Negative attitudes" towards entrepreneurs, as Scottish Enterprise found, was not "merely a reflection of wider social attitudes", but were "equally prevalent within Scottish institutions, among our teachers, policy-makers, business advisers and financiers." Little wonder, one might well exclaim, that "wider social attitudes" are so inimical to entrepreneurialism, looking at the paucity of the caste which formed them.

Scottish Enterprise has sought to claim that its strategy has not been without success, that it has changed attitudes towards entrepreneurship. But even here the evidence is ambiguous. Despite earnest endeavours to promote entrepreneurialism, a Scottish Enterprise attitude survey found a majority of people polled in 1999 still believed that government investment was more likely to lead to the creation of jobs than investment by entrepreneurs.

Nor were the poll findings much more heartening at the level of personal intention. The percentage of those saying that they "could start a business but don't want to" had barely changed at 37 per cent between 1992 and 1999. The percentage of those saying they had no interest or strong desire to start a business still stood at 69 per cent, while the proportion saying they were committed to starting a business still stood, after seven years of Scottish Enterprise endeavours, at a derisory 2.4 per cent of respondents (see charts 4 and 5). In the defeated but bleakly realistic words of Scottish Enterprise's own assessment: "The dominant theme from these results is how little attitudes have changed since the mid 1990s."[6]

A culture hostile to risk

As influential in contemporary public attitudes towards entrepreneurship has been a pervasive and relentless demonisation of risk right across an ever-widening spectrum of social action and behaviour in Britain. Almost every adversity and setback in modern life and especially in employment and the business environment, is seen as some-

[6]*Improving the Business Birth Rate*: How far we've come, pages 6-11 Scottish Enterprise, 2000

thing to be legislated against and/or compensated for. Government inspectorates and regulatory quangos have mushroomed in a culture that has supplanted action, enterprise and risk-taking with an obsession to assess, monitor and evaluate. The latter are often confused with genuine productive work and the wealth-creation process. Monitoring, assessing and evaluating have taken over from actually doing.

This is a mindless perversion of in the name of consumer or employee "protection" in which governments are in business to regulate, curtail and to prosecute, and business is in business to be regulated, curtailed and sued. Few developments in modern life have been more evocative of the era of religious intolerance and the drumming out of heretics than the politically correct harnessing of risk, work and employment. The taking of risk and the creation of value and work are not seen as having their own particular problems, still less as achievements, but as activities to be saddled with agendas ranging from environmen-

tal protection to ethnic and gender rights. When the prevailing orthodoxy is so hostile to risk and the risk taker - those in short who are to be constantly regulated and legislated against, often for no other purpose than the perception of government "busyness" – it should be no surprise that so few want to take on the responsibility of business start-up. Indeed, our only cause for surprise is that so many still choose to do so.

The myth of the engineered entrepreneur

As Scottish Enterprise itself notes in its report last year, "the fact that the negative attitudes towards entrepreneurs in Scotland have hardly shifted over the last seven years perhaps provides the best illustration of how difficult the task is of engineering an entrepreneurial renaissance."[7]

The word "engineering" is significant in this context. Indeed, it goes to the heart of the debate about government approaches which attempt to simulate

[7]The Scottish Business Birth Rate Inquiry 2000 Report, April 2000, p.20

or "manufacture" enterprise: whether entrepreneurialism can be engineered by government intervention and without regard to the general economic climate in which such engineering takes place.

One cannot help gain the impression from Scottish Enterprise brochures of a sterilised laboratory in which technicians with white aprons, rubber gloves and test tubes seek to create the ideal type sanitised Scottish Enterprise 'brochure entrepreneur'. This mythical creature is adventurous (but fully Inland Revenue and VAT compliant); job creating (but familiar with IR35, employment regulation, the 35 hour week and maternity leave); hard working (but fully mindful of statutory rest breaks and stress counselling); business hungry (but compliant with latest additions to consumer protection and EU directives); versatile (but not a plumber or in any other male-dominated occupation); innovative (but fully familiar with the requirements of non domestic rates and the assessment and appeals procedure and all key planning and building regulations); individualist (but a graduate cum laude of the local Social Exclusion monitoring unit). The model entrepreneur is a photogenic replica and clone of a Scottish Enterprise "learning experience". Such entrepreneurs do not exist outside the designer brochures of Scottish Enterprise. They cannot be factory manufactured to government specification in this way. Such engineering knocks the heart out of entrepreneurship. It misses the point completely.

Government agencies can announce impressive sounding "packages" for new business start-up schemes but the money is rendered useless if business rates and taxes are hiked and the costs of employment blindly raised by layer upon layer of regulation. Scottish Enterprise has set about its work as if this wider picture is irrelevant and as if entrprepreneurialism is something like a foreign language or business skill set that can be acquired through simulated enterprise learning experiences. But how can an agency, so obeisant to every passing whim of political correctness and comprised of enterprise officers (often local government workers put through a retread) teach entrepreneurialism? It is like asking the General Synod to hold seminars in erotica.

Basic questions to be asked

The encouragement of business start-up requires some basic questions to be asked, and Scottish Enterprise seldom seems to have asked them. For example, why do people go into business at all? They do so for a wide variety of reasons. But ultimately, they must make a profit. And the more obstacles out in the way of profit – such as tax, regulation and the non-domestic rate (now accounting for 13 per cent of the overheads of a small business) – the weaker the motivation to launch out. Yet the enterprise agencies do not seem to have made the imperative connection between these basic truths and what the rest of government does.

No one doubts Scottish Enterprise means well. But in the objectives it has set itself it has manifestly failed. It has chosen the wrong target, the wrong approach and its work is nullified by other departments of government. It produces attractive brochures on promoting entrepreneurialism, which is not the same thing as promoting entrepreneurialism. Its approach reeks of gesture politics. And its gesture of calling in the Fraser of Allander Institute to undertake a review is no substitute at all for a fully independent and impartial enquiry into what has gone wrong, why it has gone wrong, and what should now be done. Such an enquiry should not baulk from a discussion of the view that if the policy aim is to promote small business formation in Scotland, Scottish Enterprise is best wound up and its £500 million a year budget used to slash the business rate. Indeed, such a proposal, if effected, would reduce the rate burden on business in Scotland by almost 40 per cent at a stroke.

In addition to an independent enquiry and audit of the effectiveness of the current business start-up strategy and how small business start-ups could be better promoted (and more realistic objectives set), this Institute paper focuses on two areas of acute concern among small firms. These are reform of the non-domestic rate, and action to lighten the regulatory burden on business.

On business rate reform, there is a powerful case, as set out by Jim and Margaret Cuthbert, for scrapping the business rate altogether. As their paper makes clear, this option is not in the gift of the Scottish parliament. Any decision would have to be taken at UK level and would need to be accompanied by an increase in some other form of business taxation, most probably Corporation Tax.

Gerry Dowds, of the Forum of Private Business, sets out the case for moving the basis of a local business tax from the physical size of the premises to an alternative basis (such as turnover or profit) which more appropriately reflects the firm's ability to pay.

On the question of business regulation, Alastair Balfour warns that many SMEs are now on the point of "significant rebellion" over the burden of time-consuming paperwork. We may well be approaching a point where ever more regulation creates its own antidote: a general culture of non-compliance, similar to that in continental countries such as France and Italy, where the government sanctions ever more business regulation but turns a blind eye to enforcement. The danger of such a culture is that what starts as a selective non-compliance spreads to a general indifference to and contempt for, the legislative and tax gathering process: all rules become irksome, nonsensical, unenforceable. Liberal reformers may claim that it is impossible to go back, or that it is too late for business to start complaining now. On the contrary. History teaches us that it is never too late to change, only that the cost of delay keeps going up.

Bill Jamieson
Director, Policy Institute

The Business Birth Rate: Scotland's Achilles Heel

Professor Sir Donald MacKay

Executive Summary

One: Business births and deaths

Two: Business finance in Scotland

Three: Policy implications

Executive summary

This paper reviews the evidence on business birth rates and the growth performance of small and medium sized establishments (SMEs) in Scotland and considers whether the observed entrepreneurial deficit is due to difficulties in securing loan and equity finance. Its key findings are:

● Scotland lags Britain in business density

Business density (measured by the number of VAT registered businesses per 10,000 resident population) has increased in Scotland over the period 1980-99, but remains significantly below the average for Great Britain (GB). In relative terms, the position has changed very little over this period.

● London and the South East pulling away

Within this aggregate picture, business density in Scotland has risen compared with GB excluding London and the South East (LSE). But it has fallen compared with the LSE, an area which displays a high and increasing level of business density.

● Scots near the bottom of the table

In 1999, Scotland had a lower business density than all other GB regions, save only Merseyside and North East England.

● Business deficit widens with growth

Relative to its resident population, both the business birth rate and the business death rate are lower for Scotland than GB over 1980-99, but the cyclical pattern of births (and the net change in business density) follow fairly closely on that for GB. However, when the economy is expanding rapidly, the gap in birth rate (and the net change in business density) widens, and the contrast with LSE becomes more acute.

● Central belt is where the problem lies

Rural Scotland (that is, all areas outside the Central Belt) has a high birth rate by GB standards and this matches the birth rate achieved in most rural areas of GB. The entrepreneurial deficit is a Central Belt phenomenon.

● A smaller share of high growth firms

Scotland has a lower share of high growth businesses, but this appears to be due to the low business birth rate and not to a comparative failure to develop high growth businesses from a given number of business starts.

● Average deal size smaller in Scotland

Scotland's share of companies which attract private venture capital funding is higher than her share of VAT registered businesses. But the latter is close to Scotland's share of the value of venture capital invested i.e. the average deal size in Scotland is smaller than the GB average.

● Fewer MBO deals

Smaller deal size reflects the greater

prominence of early stage and expansion deals in Scotland and a much smaller representation of management buy out/management buy in (MBO/MBI) deals which are more capital intensive. This suggests that any equity gap will be less significant in Scotland.

● Lack of deals in services

The industrial spread of venture capital investment indicates that the chief weakness is a lack of deals in tradeable services, a rapidly expanding sector of the UK economy. This appears to reflect a structural weakness in the Scottish economy – a poor representation of such businesses – rather than a financial market failure.

● Big questions over public funds

Scotland has a high representation of public sector or public sector assisted funds established to assist new and growing businesses. These funds have ranged from professionally managed funds, such as Scottish Development Finance (SDF), to a large number of relatively small funds, mainly regional in their scope. The cost effectiveness of the latter appears highly questionable.

● Business angels on the rise . . .

In recent years there has been a substantial increase in business angel activity, providing a more informal channel for private funding and, often, a more 'hands on' approach to business development.

● Venture capitalists responsive

Attracting equity funding to high tech businesses may present a particular problem, but this may reflect a greater reluctance by the business owner to part with equity. On the evidence, however, the venture capital industry appears to have adapted well to the particular needs of Scottish business.

● Finance barrier declining in importance

Scottish Enterprise survey evidence indicates that the perceived difficulty of accessing finance is identified in Scotland, England and Wales, Germany and the United States as the main problem in starting a business. There is little inter-country variation in the percentage of respondents identifying this problem. Over time, in Scotland, this barrier appears to have diminished in importance and only 10 per cent who actually approached a bank for funding, reported the bank response as discouraging.

Why small business matters especially to Scotland

It is commonly assumed that, because there is a lower business density in Scotland and a lower rate of business start-up, SMEs are less important relative to business as a whole. In fact, small business matters more. According to the latest DTI statistics, there were 233,400 small and medium sized businesses in Scotland at the start of 1999. Together they employed 1.49 million or just over 60 per cent of those employed in all businesses. This SME employment share in Scotland compares with 58 per cent in the South East of England, 54 per cent in England and 42.5 per cent in London. In terms of turnover, SMEs account for 55 per cent of total business turnover in Scotland. This compares with 50 per cent in England and 47 per cent for both London and the South East regions. SMEs are therefore a more, not less important part of the business constituency in Scotland from an economic and policy-making point of view.

Policy implications

● A 'significant entrepreneurial deficit'

Business density has increased in Scotland. But Scotland continues to have a significant entrepreneurial deficit compared with GB as a whole and, particularly, with London and the South East.

● No evidence of a funding gap . . .

There is no evidence that this entrepreneurial deficit is due to a failure on the part of the financial institutions operating in Scotland – on the evidence, any equity or loan gap in Scotland is less serious than in the rest of GB.

● . . . or barriers to entry for lenders

The three major Scottish banks have a dominant position in the market for small business lending, but there is no evidence that this results in an inferior service to business clients. Moreover, the evolution of the systems which control small business lending and the decreasing importance of the branch network in this process, make the market for small business loans more contestable for other banks. The lack of other contestants is more likely to be due to the limited profitability of the business, rather than to barriers to entry.

● Equity and loan funding 'not a problem'

The evidence does not support the proposition that the entrepreneurial gap in Scotland is due to particular problems in obtaining equity and loan funding. Compared with the rest of GB, Scottish businesses are well served in terms of access to equity and loan funding.

● Cultural factors may hold the key

The entrepreneurial deficit remains a matter of concern, but it appears to be historical, sociological and cultural, not financial in origin.

How micro businesses are big players

Micro businesses (defined as those employing between one and ten people) are frequently overlooked in government policymaking, their voice often drowned out by the big battalions of the Confederation of British Industry. Yet in aggregate they have a huge macro impact on the UK economy.

These micro businesses account for 94.7 per cent of the total business population, 21 per cent of total business turnover, and 31 per cent of total employment.

Taking the wider definition of small business - firms employing up to 99 people, the figures are even more startling. There are 3.7 million in total. And they account for 99 per cent of the total business population, 44 per cent of total turnover and 51 per cent of the total employed in business.

The total number of firms registered for VAT is 1.6 million. This suggests more than half of all small business go unrecorded in many business monitoring statistics and opinion surveys. Large businesses (those with 500 or more employees) often cede the argument on the burden of ever rising workplace regulation as it is a proportionately much smaller addition to costs and they are better able to cope. But these businesses account for barely a third (36 per cent) of all employees in business and represent just 0.2 per cent of total businesses in the UK.

1: Business births and deaths

[8]Employment Gazette, November 1991
[9]*Scotland's Business Birth Rate*, Scottish Enterprise and Scottish Business Insider, 1994

• The exclusion of businesses below the VAT threshold is a major omission in current policy analysis. It is probable that the business stock in Scotland may contain a relatively higher share of businesses with a turnover below the VAT threshold. It may be argued that the limited scale of these businesses means that they will not make a major contribution to income or employment creation, or that they are a significant source of high growth businesses. However, until research is undertaken we do not know for sure. Small business below the VAT threshold may not be 'significant' employers in the statistical sense, but they are users and consumers of other business services in their local areas and thus have a significant indirect impact on employment overall.

Introduction

The period since the 1970s has seen a growing recognition of the importance of the small business sector and a high business birth rate in determining economic growth rates. A number of authors (for example, Daly, Campbell, Robson and Gallaghar[8]) have shown that small businesses have accounted for a disproportionately large share of net new job creation in the period from the 1970s. This has been the product of a high rate of 'churn', that is, both a high rate of new venture formation and a high death rate. Thus, almost one-half of all new ventures do not survive beyond 10 years (this period may be as short as 5 years) and a high proportion of these business 'deaths' occur in the first 2.5 years (Ganguly).

Research undertaken by Scottish Enterprise[9] shows that while the number of businesses registered in Scotland increased over 1980-90, both the business birth rate and the stock of businesses relative to the resident population was substantially lower for Scotland than for the rest of the UK. Further, it was considered that the low business birth rate was a major factor in the relatively poor performance of the Scottish economy and that an increase in the birth rate should be a major objective of public policy. Here, I revisit that analysis to see whether the same conclusions still apply in the 1990s. The short answer is that the stock of businesses in Scotland has increased, but the 'entrepreneurial deficit' in Scotland relative to Great Britain as a whole, remains much as it was at the beginning of the 1980s.

Our analysis is based primarily on statistics relating to VAT-registered busi-

Chart 1: Scots business start-ups on the slide

Business start-ups less involuntary closures: net

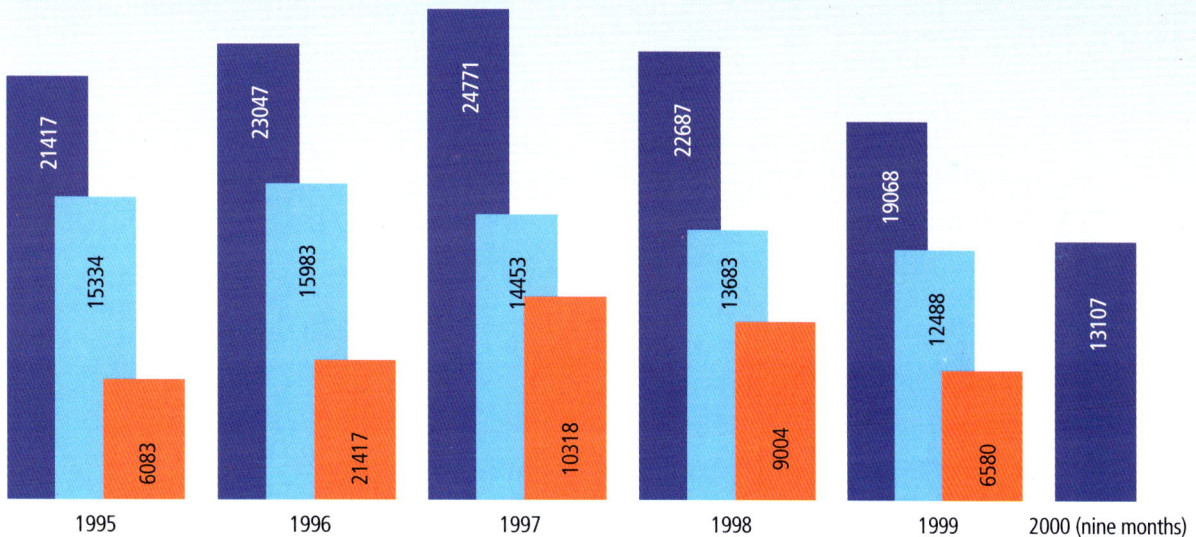

	1995	1996	1997	1998	1999	2000 (nine months)
Dark blue	21417	23047	24771	22687	19068	13107
Light blue	15334	15983	14453	13683	12488	
Orange	6083	21417	10318	9004	6580	

New business start-ups in Scotland peaked in 1997. By 1999 the annual rate of business starts fell below that of 1995, the first year of he statistical run. The figure of 13,107 for the first nine months of 2000 is 12.4 per cent down on the comparable period of 1999.

Chart 2: Scotland's enterprise deficit

New VAT registrations per 10,000 population

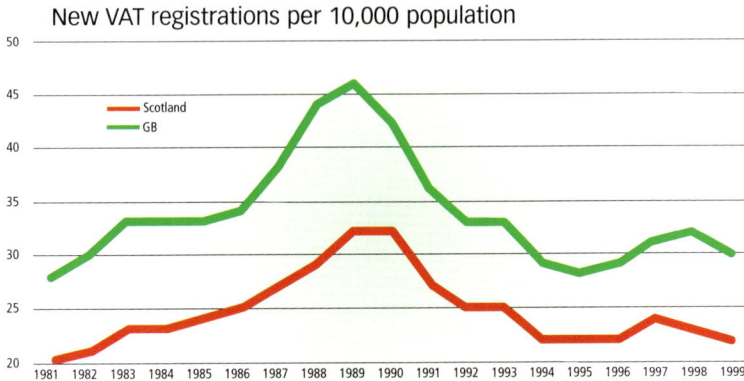

The graph shows how new VAT registrations per 10,000 population in Scotland consistently lag the figure for GB. This is the "enterprise deficit". See Professor Sir Donald MacKay's paper for detailed analysis.

Chart 3: How business start-ups track economic growth

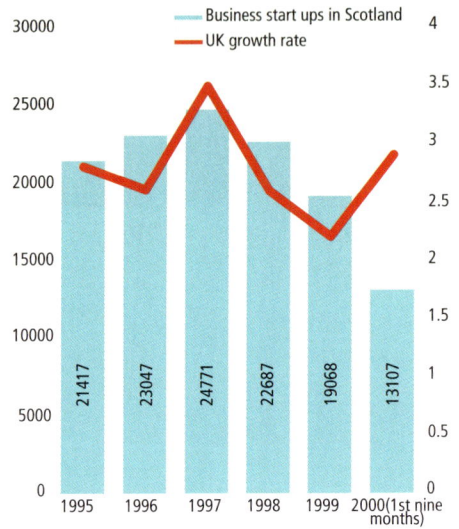

Chart 4: Attitudes to enterprise: who's really trading places

Chart 5: Scotland's attitude deficit

Attitudes to entrepreneurship, MORI poll, 1999

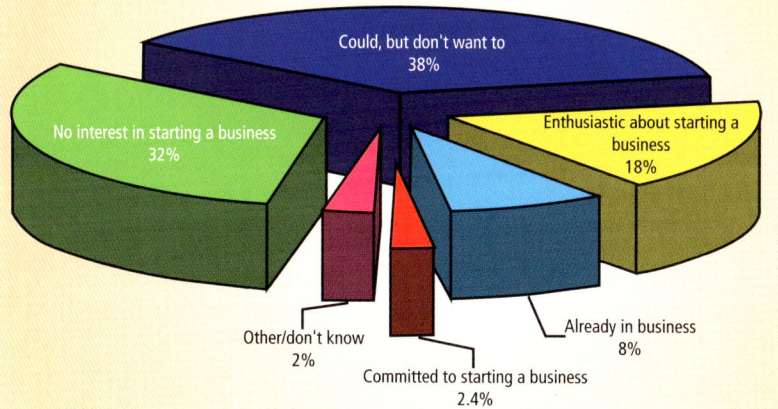

Could, but don't want to
38%

No interest in starting a business
32%

Enthusiastic about starting a business
18%

Other/don't know
2%

Committed to starting a business
2.4%

Already in business
8%

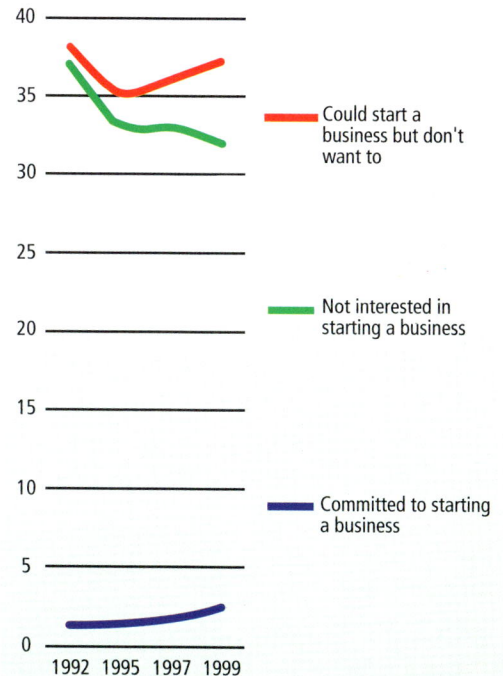

Could start a business but don't want to

Not interested in starting a business

Committed to starting a business

1992 1995 1997 1999

Despite eight years of unbroken economic growth, most Scots still do not want to go into business. Note the tiny percentage of those saying they are committed to starting a business (2.4%)

Attitudes to entrepreneurship have been tracked since 1992 with a biennial survey carried out by MORI on behalf of Scottish Enterprise. SE says there is evidence of change, but as the graph shows, it is neither dramatic nor compelling

Chart 11: Net survivors: We miss the peaks - but avoid the troughs

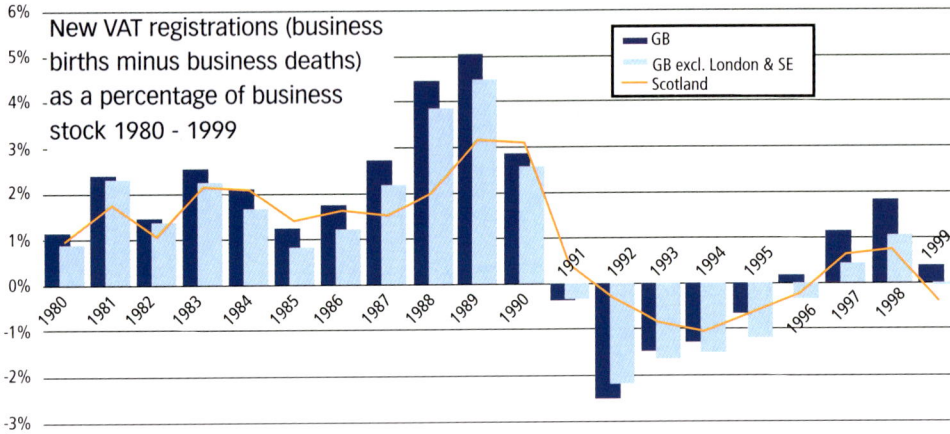

New VAT registrations (business births minus business deaths) as a percentage of business stock 1980 - 1999

Legend:
- GB
- GB excl. London & SE
- Scotland

Note how Scots net business creation rate falls short of the peaks, but avoids the worst of the slumps

Chart 10: The belt that holds us down

Note the distinct, and persistent, low business density in the Central Belt area

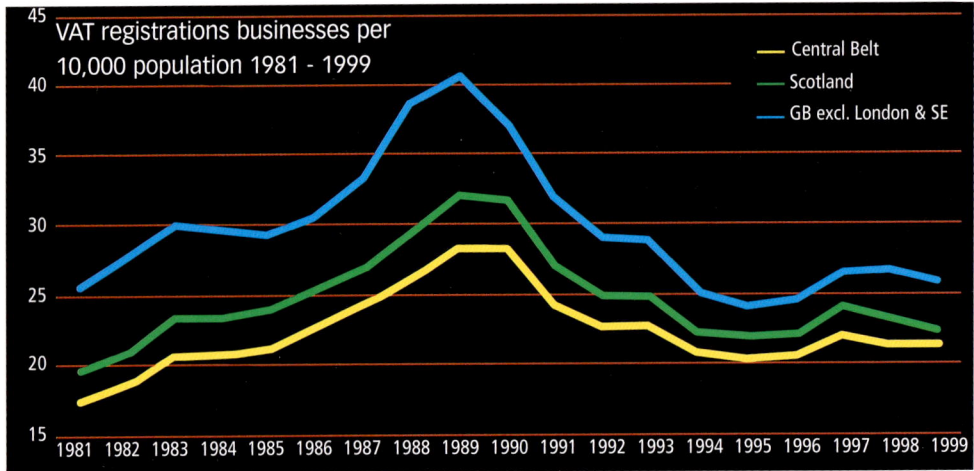

VAT registrations businesses per 10,000 population 1981 - 1999

Legend:
- Central Belt
- Scotland
- GB excl. London & SE

Chart 6: The business stock scorecard 1981–1999: how Scotland compares

VAT registered businesses per 10,000 population 1981–99

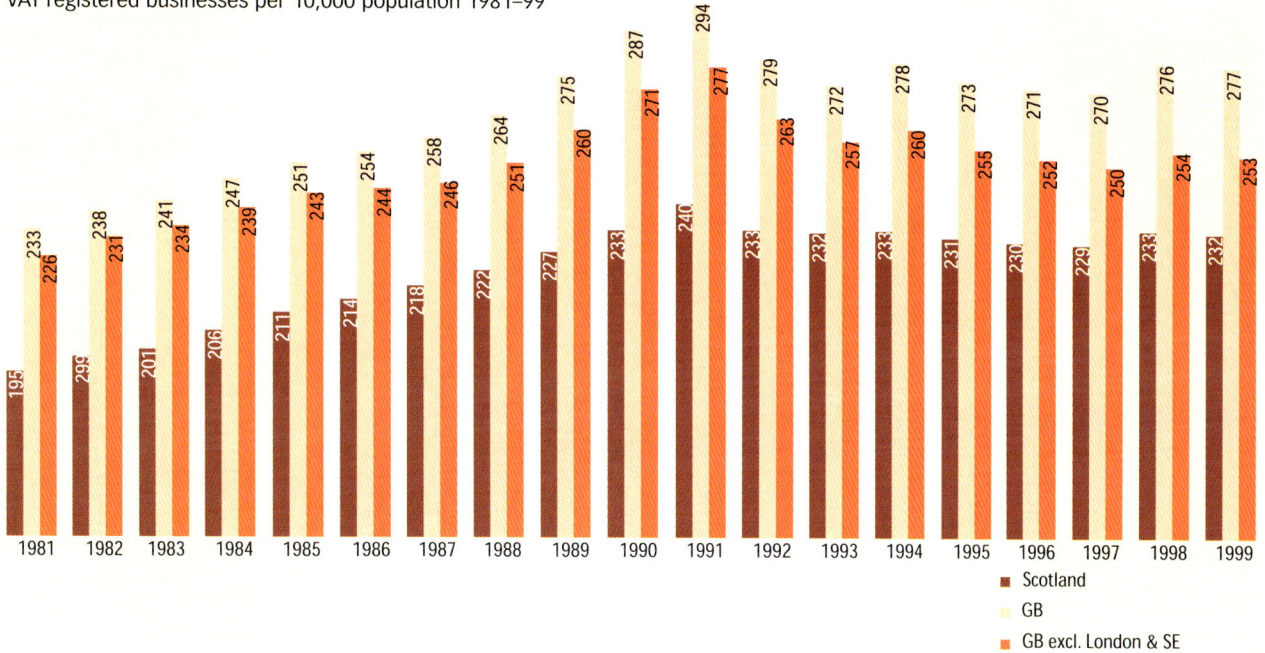

Note how business density improved in Scotland in the early years from 1981 to 1990, but then flattened off. See also the gap in business density has hardly changed between Scotland and GB, but has notably narrowed with the rest of GB ex London and the South east.

Chart 7: The enterprise deficit: Scotland's lower business density

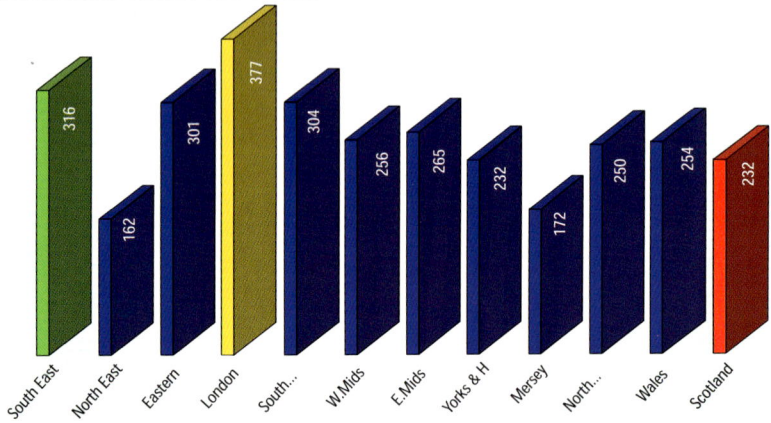

Note the high business densities in London and the South East compared with other regions. The average for GB as a whole is 227 per 10,00 population. London, with, 377, is 36 per cent above average,Scotland, with 232, is 16 per cent below

Bars: South East 316, North East 162, Eastern 301, London 377, South... 304, W.Mids 256, E.Mids 265, Yorks & H 232, Mersey 172, North... 250, Wales 254, Scotland 232

Chart 14: Business births: how Scotland trails the GB average

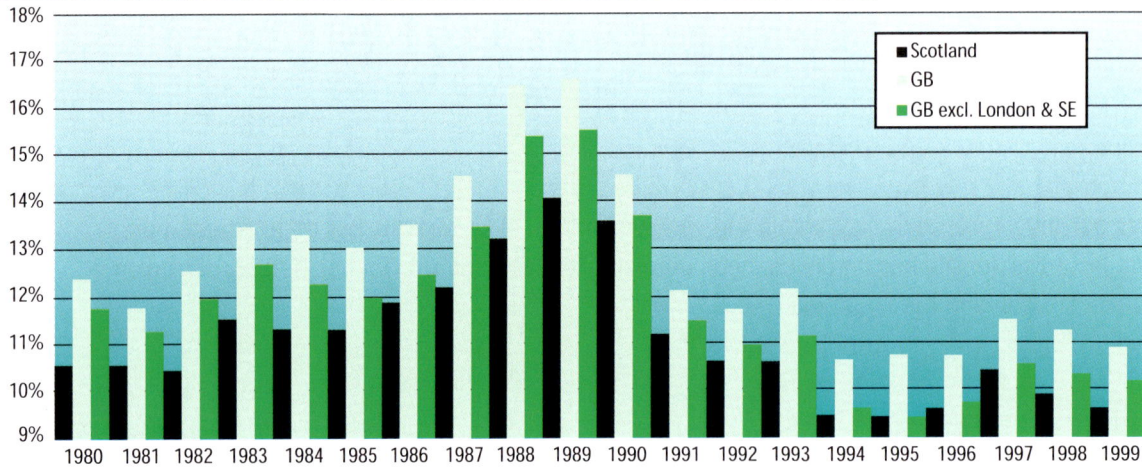

Legend: Scotland, GB, GB excl. London & SE

The chart shows the business birth rate for Scotland, GB and GB excluding London and the South East since 1980. Note how the Scottish business birth rate has been lower than the GB average – but the difference has narrowed slightly in the 1990s

Chart 8: VAT registered businesses per 10,000 population, 1981–1999

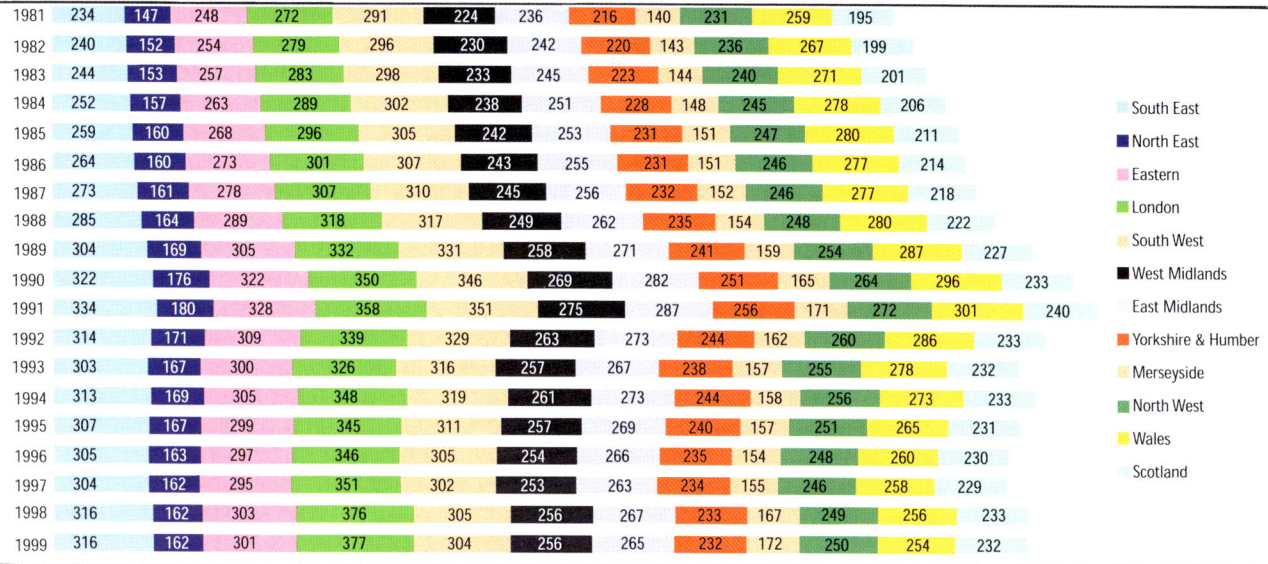

Year	South East	North East	Eastern	London	South West	West Midlands	East Midlands	Yorkshire & Humber	Merseyside	North West	Wales	Scotland
1981	234	147	248	272	291	224	236	216	140	231	259	195
1982	240	152	254	279	296	230	242	220	143	236	267	199
1983	244	153	257	283	298	233	245	223	144	240	271	201
1984	252	157	263	289	302	238	251	228	148	245	278	206
1985	259	160	268	296	305	242	253	231	151	247	280	211
1986	264	160	273	301	307	243	255	231	151	246	277	214
1987	273	161	278	307	310	245	256	232	152	246	277	218
1988	285	164	289	318	317	249	262	235	154	248	280	222
1989	304	169	305	332	331	258	271	241	159	254	287	227
1990	322	176	322	350	346	269	282	251	165	264	296	233
1991	334	180	328	358	351	275	287	256	171	272	301	240
1992	314	171	309	339	329	263	273	244	162	260	286	233
1993	303	167	300	326	316	257	267	238	157	255	278	232
1994	313	169	305	348	319	261	273	244	158	256	273	233
1995	307	167	299	345	311	257	269	240	157	251	265	231
1996	305	163	297	346	305	254	266	235	154	248	260	230
1997	304	162	295	351	302	253	263	234	155	246	258	229
1998	316	162	303	376	305	256	267	233	167	249	256	233
1999	316	162	301	377	304	256	265	232	172	250	254	232

Note the "swelling out" of London and South East areas over the years, while Scotland has remained relatively static

Chart 9: Familiar theme, seven different keys

Overall, business density, as measured by number of business per 10,000 population, has risen in all regions since 1981. But who says there isn't a North-South divide?

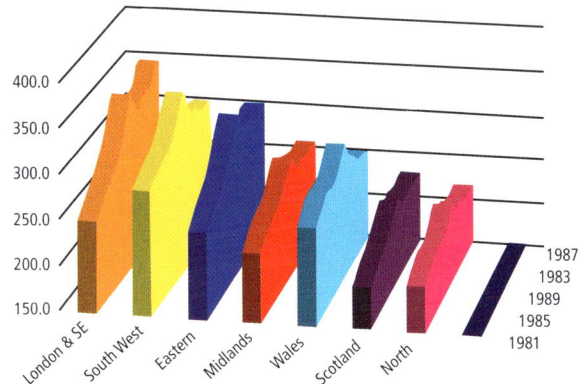

Chart 12: Fewer companies caught in the death web

VAT deregistrations per 10,000 population, 1981–1999

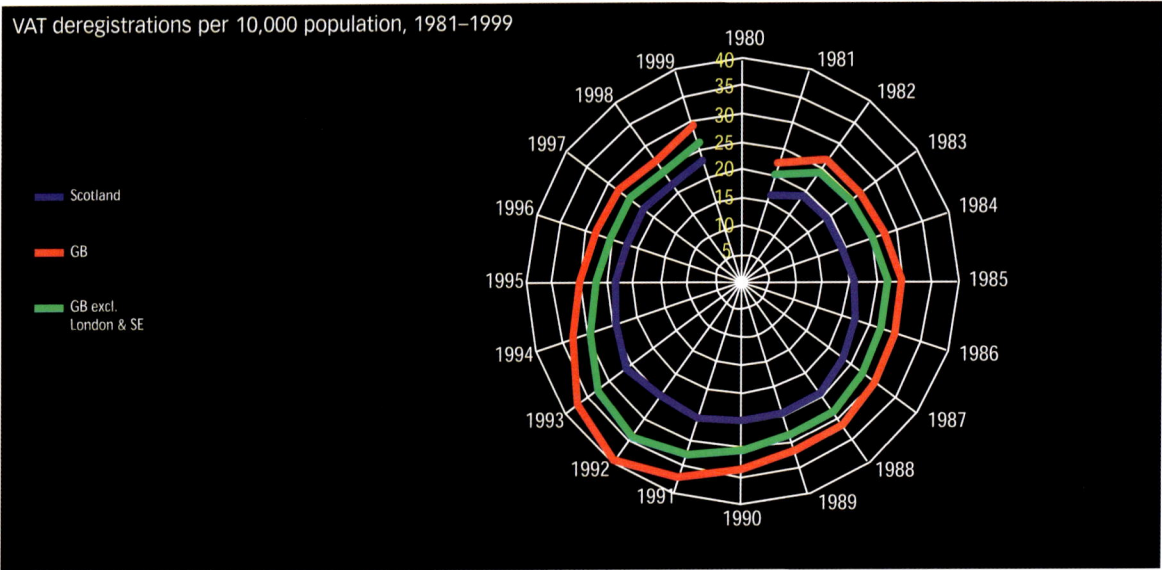

Legend:
- Scotland
- GB
- GB excl. London & SE

The closer to the centre of the spider's web, the lower the company death rate.

New VAT registration, 1999

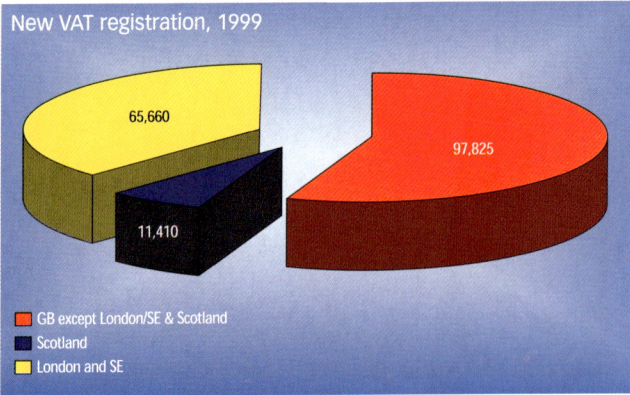

- 65,660
- 11,410
- 97,825

- GB except London/SE & Scotland
- Scotland
- London and SE

Chart 13: 1999 new company hatches, by region

Note the size of London and the South East in relation to GB

nesses. Although this data source excludes businesses whose turnover is below the VAT threshold (this accounting for most self-employed persons), it is by far the most comprehensive source of information on the business stock.

The business stock

The best single measure of business density is the number of VAT registered businesses per 10,000 of the population. **Chart 6** shows this measure for Scotland, Great Britain (GB), and GB excluding London and the South East (LSE), for 1981-99.

During this period, business density increased in Scotland, from 195 VAT registered businesses per 10,000 population in 1981, to 232 per 10,000 in 1999. This increase was concentrated in the period to 1991. Since then, business density in Scotland has shown no significant change. Throughout the period, the relative position in Scotland compared with GB as a whole has been remarkably stable. In 1980 the Scottish density per 10,000 population (195) was 83.7 per cent of the GB average (233). In 1999 the Scottish density (232) was 83.6 per cent of the GB average (277).

The business stock rose in all areas shown in chart 1 (this holding true for a more disaggregated analysis) but the relativities changed very little. Hence, if, in GB terms, Scotland suffered from an entrepreneurial gap in 1981, much the same could be concluded in 1999.

A finer regional analysis reveals one critical factor to be carefully evaluated in analysing Scottish outcomes. The judgement of relative performance is decisively influenced by whether London and South East (LSE) is included or excluded from the relevant comparator. LSE is easily the largest UK region. It has a high business density, and this has increased substantially since the early 1980s. If it is the comparator, then the entrepreneurial deficit in Scotland has increased over time. If it is included in the comparator (say the comparator is GB), then the entrepreneurial deficit has hardly changed. If it is excluded from the comparator, then the entrepreneurial deficit has diminished through time.

Charts 7 and 8 show business density by region in 1999 and over the period 1981 to 1999 respectively. Evidently, business densities are high in the south and the east of England and low in the north and west of GB. This general pattern has been stable throughout the period from 1981, as demonstrated by chart 2b. Scotland emerges as a region where the business density has increased, in absolute terms, since 1981. But compared with most other regions, business density has remained relatively low. In **chart 9**, which provides a more aggregative overview, only the north of England (NW and NE combined) has a lower business density by the end of the period.

Now consider the wider comparators. The figures quoted earlier show that, over 1981-99, there was very little change in Scottish business density relative to that in GB as a whole. However, if the comparison is between the Scottish business density and that of GB excluding London and the South East, then it remains absolutely lower in Scotland - but the gap has narrowed. In 1981, business density in Scotland was just over 86 per cent of the GB figure excluding LSE, but rose to just under 92 per cent by 1999.

What really stands out in chart 3, however, is that business density was high in London and the South East in 1981 and rose particularly rapidly over 1981-99. Because of its weight, LSE is clearly the most important GB region and the comparison with Scotland is instructive. In 1981, the Scottish business density per 10,000 population (195) was 77 per cent of the business density of LSE (253); in 1999 the Scottish density (232) was only 67 per cent of the LSE density (345). If business density is an important factor in determining the growth dynamics of a region, then Scotland has lost ground to LSE particularly, has held its own relative to GB as a whole, and has gained ground on GB excluding LSE.

The other interesting feature is that

SCOTLAND'S ENTERPRISE DEFICIT

business density varies very substantially within Scotland itself and, indeed, within the other standard regions of GB. Grampian, the Orkneys and the Shetlands all emerge as areas with high business density, and business density in the Highlands and in the south of Scotland matches many areas in the south and east of England.

So, if there is an entrepreneurial deficit in Scotland, it is confined to the densely populated Central Belt. Once again this is a long standing problem, whose main features have changed relatively little over time. To illustrate this, **chart 10** shows changes in business density for the Central Belt and for Rural Scotland (all of Scotland outside the Central Belt) and compares these outcomes with GB excluding LSE over 1981-99. The Central Belt has a much lower business density than other areas of GB, even when LSE is excluded. By contrast, business density is high in rural Scotland.

The relatively low business density in Scotland is, therefore, a Central Belt phenomenon. Other parts of Great Britain which do have particularly low business densities, such as the North East of England, South Wales, Merseyside and South Yorkshire, and the larger conurbations, such as Birmingham, Manchester, Cardiff and Bristol. The important exception is London where business density is high. It seems inherently implausible that the financial sector is the main driver of the observed differences.

Business Birth Rates

How has this outcome in Scotland been affected by the business birth rate and the death rate? The business birth rate can be defined in two ways: annual VAT registrations as a percentage of the business stock, or annual VAT registrations per 10,000 population.

These definitions provide rather different perspectives. The former shows business births as a percentage of the number of businesses (the business stock) and the latter business births as a percentage of the resident population.

If the Scottish birth rate relative to the number of businesses is increasing, then the stock of businesses is increasing more rapidly in Scotland. Yet, starting from a position with a small stock of businesses (as is the case in Scotland) a rising birth rate in this respect might still be consistent with a lower birth rate relative to the resident population, which requires analysing registrations per 10,000 population.

VAT registrations as percentage of business stock: **Chart 11** shows the business birth rate for Scotland, Great Britain, and Great Britain excluding LSE over 1980-1999. Over the whole period, the Scottish business birth rate relative to the business stock was lower than the British average, but that difference narrowed slightly in the 1990s.

The same holds true for the comparison with GB excluding LSE. By the end of the 1990s, the business birth rate relative to the business stock was much the same for Scotland and for the rest of GB outside LSE (although still lower than for GB as a whole because of the influence of LSE).

VAT Registrations per 10,000 Population: I now consider the business birth rate defined in terms of the number of VAT registrations per 10,000 population. While there is a clear cyclical pattern for all areas, with a high business birth rate in the late 1980s and a decline thereafter, the relativities between the different areas again show a high degree of stability. The only exception is the boom in business births in the later 1980s, which was much more marked outside Scotland, and, particularly, in LSE.

Business Death Rates

As with birth rates, business deregistration or 'death' rates, in terms of VAT deregistrations, can be defined in two ways: VAT deregistrations as a percentage of the business stock, or VAT deregistrations per 10,000 population.

Businesses may deregister for a number of reasons, not all of which result from business failure. A deregistration may result from retirement of the owner, or takeover by another company, a change in legal status (for example, incorporation) or a fall in turnover which takes the business below the VAT threshold. As such, business failure is only one of many possible reasons for VAT deregistration. Nonetheless, business failure is the chief cause of deregistration and the deregulation data do provide an indication of the general trends in business failures, offering the advantage of comparability over time and across sub-regions of Great Britain.

VAT Deregistrations as percentage of Business Stock: Here chart 12 tells a straightforward message: the death rate of businesses in Scotland is lower than in the GB as a whole, and than in GB excluding LSE. There is, therefore, less 'churn' in the business population in Scotland, because of a lower birth rate and a lower death rate.

VAT Deregistrations per 10,000 stock: The same conclusion, that Scotland has a lower business 'death' rate as well as a lower birth rate, emerges when the death rate is defined per 10,000 resident population . The two events appear likely to be related, in that a high birth rate is likely to be associated with a high death rate and vice-versa.

Net Vat Registrations: The change in the business stock and in business density is, of course, the net outcome of two large flows - a flow of new business start-ups (registrations) and a flow of businesses which cease trading (deregistrations). It is useful to net out these gross flows to establish the net effect - this will result in the incoming stock of businesses and higher business density when new registrations exceed deregistrations and vice versa. The net flow will tend to be positive (or greater) when economic conditions are favourable (and vice-versa).

Here I concentrate on the net birth rate over 1980-99 (starts less deaths as a percentage of the business stock). As would be expected from previous analysis, the net birth rate follows the same general pattern in each area. However, the cyclical pattern is damped for Scotland and more subject to cyclical fluctuation than for GB, mainly because of the influence of LSE.

In the 1980s the net birth rate was lowest in Scotland, even although Scotland started from a low base. In contrast, through most of the 1990s, the increase in the net birth rate relative to the business stock has been greatest in Scotland. Given the pattern of changes it appears unlikely that a secular shift has occurred. Rather, these differences appear to reflect cyclical factors. In the mid and late 1980s, Scotland lagged the strong economic growth of the GB economy. In the early and mid-1990s Scotland suffered less from the slow down in economic growth. By the end of the 1990s relative positions had changed little compared with the early 1980s, although in all areas business density has increased.

High growth business

It is widely accepted that the changing nature of the economy has enhanced the importance of an entrepreneurial society characterised by, amongst other things, a high business birth rate. The evidence is that this is necessarily accompanied by a high death rate. In short, the small business sector evolves through a Darwinian process of selection, which weeds out the failures early in life. Hence, some 50 per cent of new businesses cease trading within a 10 year period (it has been suggested that this period may be as short as 5 years) and the great bulk of the survivors remain small businesses through all of their life cycle.

Nonetheless, it is also widely accepted that, from this high birth rate and death rate, a few very high growth businesses will emerge and will be very important in generating income and employment growth in the economy as a whole. The issue that now has to be considered is whether these high growth businesses are more or less prevalent in Scotland.

The evidence is that Scotland does appear to have a low share of high growth or high performance businesses, largely as a consequence of the low business birth rate. Research undertaken for Scottish Enterprise, using Dun and Bradstreet data for 1978-90 and 1985-97 as a base, found that as a percentage of new business starts, Scotland had a higher number of high growth businesses than the West Midlands and South East England (the former taken to represent an average region and the latter the best performing region). However, adjusting for population size, the number of high growth business was significantly lower in Scotland than for both the West Midlands and South East England. The conclusion reached by Scottish Enterprise was:

"There is a strong connection between the business birth rate and the generation of faster-growing businesses. Areas that produce the highest numbers of fast-growing businesses, like South East England, also tend to have the highest rates of business start-up. It seems that increasing the number of fast-growing companies is strongly dependent on the need to have a high business birth rate overall. "

This conclusion is supported by research carried out by Mason. He found, on the basis of a population of 1,000 businesses with the highest growth rates listed in the Growth Companies Register, that new businesses demonstrating rapid growth were concentrated in urban regions, particularly in Greater London and the South East (44% of the total), Yorkshire and West Humberside (11%) and North West England (10%). Only Strathclyde in Scotland had any significant representation of high growth businesses. Again, an analysis of SMEs joining the Unlisted Securities Market, showed 59% located in the South East. Scotland, Wales, Northern Ireland and the North of England all had low representations.

Conclusions

The evidence is that Scotland has a low business birth rate and, largely because it has a low business birth rate, Scotland is also poorly represented amongst high growth SMEs. In short, because the birth rate of new businesses is low, there is only a small population of new businesses from which to develop high growth companies. Over the period 1981-99, business density has increased in Scotland (from 195 to 232 businesses per 10,000 population) but the relative position to GB has remained remarkably stable. Within that overall stability, Scotland's business density has improved to the rest of GB excluding LSE, but fallen further compared to LSE. Of course, as our analysis demonstrates, the low business birth rate in Scotland is a phenomenon restricted to the Central Belt – it finds no echo in rural Scotland.

Scottish Enterprise has correctly identified the low business birth rate as a critical factor in determining economic performance. It remains as critical today as it was when it was first identified as a major issue. Our task in the following analysis is to consider whether the lower birth rate of businesses in Scotland is due, in whole or in part, to a greater difficulty in obtaining access to loan finance and equity capital; and, in particular, to any differences in the operation of the financial institutions in Scotland.

Changing attitudes?

Scottish Enterprise makes much of its success in changing attitudes towards entrepreneurship in Scotland. But while there has been some improvement, as one might expect after a seven year period of uninterrupted economic growth, there is little evidence that the Scottish Enterprise campaign has made much headway. The percentage of those saying they had no interest or strong desire to start a business still stands at 69 per cent (against 75 per cent previously) while those saying they are committed to starting a business are still dishearteningly low at just 2.4 per cent.

Scotland's business burden: £1.3 billion in rates

Gross income of local authorities in Scotland in 1997/98 totalled £9.6 billion. Of this, £5.3 billion (55 per cent) came from government grants. A further £1.6 billion (17 per cent) came from fees and charges (mainly council house rents). Businesses in Scotland contributed £1.3 billion (14 per cent). The balance of £1.1 billion came from council tax. As a percentage of non government revenue, businesses contribute just over 30 per cent of local government income. The two most frequent complaints of business are that they receive very little in return by way of facilities or services (businesses have to finance their own refuse collection) and that they are grossly ill represented in relation to the contribution they make.

How can we promote young entrepreneurs?

Why are there so many Scots all over the world with successful businesses – and so few here? That was the question first put by Scottish Enterprise Chief Executive Crawford Beveridge at the Business Birth Rate Inquiry in 1992. Eight years later, in February 2000, with no evident narrowing of the enterprise deficit between Scotland the rest of the UK, the inquiry forum was reconvened to consider the question afresh.

Beveridge set out the progress made since 1992. Some 4,000 university students every year are going through entrepreneurial courses, with some 13 per cent starting businesses. A total of 40,000 students (10 per cent of the total) have some form of "enterprise learning experience" in schools. New venture funds such as Scottish Equity Partnership have added more than £40 million to the pool of equity finance available. Through Business Forums and the Entrepreneurial Exchange there are now networks in place to help budding entrepreneurs. Yet we are still not where we want to be. What more needs to be done?

The forum heard contributions from entrepreneurs, venture capitalists, business people, commentators and academics. A strong theme in the discussion was the recognition that much of the potential entrepreneurship in Scotland was wrapped up in the coming generation.

To reflect this shift, it was felt Young Enterprise Scotland should continue to shift away from its traditional "corporate" model to one more suited to the modern type of small business. The work going on in schools needs to be extended, becoming a central part of the curriculum. It was felt further effort was needed to unlock the potential in science and technology within Scottish universities, which need to see themselves as "an integral part of the economy"– and a big source of potential entrepreneurs and ideas.

The entrepreneur Chris van der Kuyl

suggested that some incentive should be provided such as, for example, an extension of university loans and grants as early forms of business subsidy, perhaps involving tax incentives. Universities could also become equity-focused in terms of the support offered to graduate entrepreneurs and spin-out companies.

New business and social inclusion

More effort should be put into extending entrepreneurship into the "social inclusion" agenda – encouraging people in all social groups to be more enterprising. As **Alan Sinclair**, chief executive of the Wise Group, commented: "This is potentially a big incubation area – but currently there seem to be no eggs."

Other suggestions included learning from and adopting best practice available. For example, UK tax policy is not as competitive as it could be and lacks flexibility. In contrast, the Irish model seems to have worked.

Ian McCaig, of the Ayrshire-based tourism business Celtic Links, said that in the tourist sector the low business start-up rate was causing stagnation, with no new blood coming in. Most people entering it see it as a property investment. Others move into the industry as a career change rather than a business opportunity. There should be scope for specific action to encourage better quality start-ups.

Some suggested the setting up of an Entrepreneurial Exchange-concept organisation for younger businesses, while others felt that more could be done in schools to promote entrepreneurialism.

Questions going forward

● What further steps could be taken to encourage young people to set up in business?

● Does our education system sufficiently value entrepreneurialism? Or is there still a cultural "bias against business"?

● Do Scottish universities make best use of entrepreneurial opportunity? How can we make better use of Scotlandís reputation as a knowledge and education centre to foster new business creation in the knowledge economy?

● What more can be done to present Scotland as an "opportunity location" – a hot spot where business and enterprise flourishes?

(Taken from Scottish Business Birth Rate Inquiry 2000 Abstract of Proceedings at House for an Art Lover, February 9 2000. For further details see Scottish Enterprise website.)

2: Business finance in Scotland

Equity Finance

In the 1990s the main venture capitalists conducting business in Scotland were 3i, Ivory and Sime/Baronsmead, Abtrust Fund Managers, Dunedin Ventures, Northern Venture Managers and British Linen Securities - together they are estimated to have invested more than £100 million per annum.[10]

The British Venture Capital Association (BVCA), who represent virtually every major source of private venture capital in GB, provide the most detailed regional analysis of the spread and level of such investment (see British Venture Capital Association, 1998). Between 1984 and 1999 a total of 1,894 Scottish companies received venture capital funding. Over the whole period 1984-99, the Scottish companies that attracted venture capital funding were 11.7 per cent of the GB total. This was substantially above Scotland's share of VAT registered business in Scotland, which varied over 7.2-7.8 per cent for the same period. Hence, venture capital funding supported a relatively high percentage of the stock of Scottish businesses.

If we look at Scotland's share of the value of venture capital funding, then this is very close to her share of VAT registered businesses, suggesting that the average level of funding per case is lower in Scotland. Some element of this reflects a known bias in the data, in that the concentration of HQ functions in London skews the regional distribution (particularly of large deals) in its favour, even when these investments have a national 'spread'. However, although the precise bias cannot be identified satisfactorily, the venture capital industry in Scotland readily accepts the proposi-

[10]*Loan and Equity Funding to SMEs in Central Scotland,* Grant Thornton Scotland and Firn Crichton Roberts Ltd

tion that the average 'deal' in Scotland is appreciably smaller than the GB average. As the BVCA puts it:

"Scotland has long been a strong supporter of the early stage and of the (capital venture) market which in 1998 accounted for more than a quarter of the companies backed in Scotland (26 per cent), representing 13 per cent of all early stage companies backed in the UK."

Scotland also accounts for a relatively high share of the value of investment in business expansion funded by private venture capital (12 per cent and 11 per cent of all GB cases in 1998 and 1999 respectively). But it has had a relatively low share of management buy-out/management buy-in (MBO/MBI) activity that has accounted for an increasing share of GB activity. In 1998 and 1999, Scotland's share of such investment was only 5 per cent respectively. MBO/MBI deals, compared with most venture capital activity, is capital intensive involving a high investment per case.

Over the 1990s it appears probable that Scotland's share of total UK venture capital investment was proportionate to her employment representation in resources and consumer goods, much less than proportionate in services, and more than proportionate in utilities and facilities, and information technology. This does not suggest that businesses in Scotland have more difficulty in accessing venture capital funds than business based elsewhere in the UK. However, it does suggest that very little venture capital is going into service industries where the representation of high growth companies is substantial. This is most likely to reflect an often noted weakness in Scotland's industrial structure - a lack of businesses, particularly SMEs, engaged in tradeable services.

BVCA data show, over time, a marked progression to larger deals in GB as a whole, much of which has been due to increase MBO/MBI activity. Venture capital funds have increased in scale, but this may have reduced their appetite for smaller deals, where any equity gap is likely to be most severe. The funding problems resulting for smaller quoted companies have been exacerbated by the weakness in their share prices.

This trend will also have affected Scotland, but it is still clear that the average deal size in Scotland has remained much smaller and that Scotland has been, and still remains, well represented in early stage and expansion venture capital funding. The importance of this point is that this is particularly where the equity gap is supposed to bite. The quantitative evidence is, therefore, that the venture capital business in Scotland has probably done more to address any equity gap than the business in GB as a whole. The BVCA is of the view that:

"In Scotland, where a high proportion of registered companies succeed in raising venture capital each year, there is a higher number of venture capital firms' offices than in any other region and the financial community is renowned for its 'networking'."

A major factor in this has been the contribution of the public sector and an evolving partnership with private venture capitalists. Indeed, one of the most distinctive features of the venture capital market in Scotland is the high degree of involvement and experimentation by the public sector - effectively Scottish Enterprise, the Local Enterprise Companies (LECs) and local authorities, often backed by European Regional Development Fund finance.

The 18 main public sector and public sector assisted funds operating in Central and Eastern Scotland in 1996 had a total of £76.3 million of investment funds, of which £70 million was committed.

The longest lived and most 'professional' public sector initiative is Scottish Enterprise's equity funding body, Scottish Development Finance. It provides equity funding for some 20 cases a year and the average first-round investment is some £300,000. SDF has been subject to a number of reviews, but all have concluded that it serves a useful role in reducing the equity gap and that it is well managed, with an acceptable rate of return on the public funds invested.

Other public sector involvement in equity funding is largely through the LECs and local authorities, but the capital base of these funds is very small (seldom approaching £5 million). These schemes have been constructed to be more responsive to local needs and their rationale is that they will adopt a different risk return profile than venture capitalists. However, it has been estimated that public sector funding accounts for only 6 per cent of start-up capital requirements in Central Scotland. Moreover, a review of these initiatives did suggest:

"... that there was a downside to public sector investment in equity funding, including the possibility of political conflicts of interest, poor marketing, and the fragmentation which has lead (sic) to an overall cost base deemed to be excessive, time consuming bureaucracy,

and no common delivery points".[11]

As a general comment, provision is small scale and fragmentary, with little evidence as to impact. The most ambitious local authority scheme is the West of Scotland Loan Fund (with an initial capital of £65 million), the successor to the Strathclyde Business Loan Scheme which ended on 1 April 1996. In its last full year of operation the West of Scotland Loan Fund provided support to 120 businesses, at an average loan of £12,000. In 1996, excluding SDF, 16 different public sector and private sector assisted schemes were identified as operating in Central Scotland and these 16 schemes had total funds of some £78 million.

In recent years the major new development was the establishment of the Scottish Equity Partnership. This is an agreement between SDF and 15 private investors (mostly institutions) with a capital fund of £25 million. Its objectives are to provide mainly equity based financial packages, which might be as

[11]Grant Thornton Scotland and Firn Crichton Roberts Ltd

little as £50,000 in exceptional cases, with a target average package of £250,000. It was anticipated that it would invest along with private funds, and its target borrowers were new ventures and growth businesses, particularly in high technology, manufacturing and knowledge-based activities. The establishment of SEP was assisted by a 50 per cent guarantee from the European Investment Fund. This has been applied to the private sector's share of the fund, in effect assuring that their capital contribution is fully recoverable. SEP is a closed Limited Partnership, creating an environment in which the fund can operate without Scottish Office intervention for an initial three year period.

Public sector or public sector assisted funds have been more numerous in the West of Scotland but they are not necessarily more effective. Many of the West of Scotland funds are small with little private sector involvement in their management.

It is difficult to escape the conclusion that there is a need to review the smaller public sector led initiatives. Some seem too small to attract and retain a strong management team and there must be a serious question made as to whether the smaller funds are providing a 'value for money' service. However, it would be difficult to conclude that in Scotland there has been a reluctance to recognise the possibility that an equity gap may be inhibiting the birth or development of high growth businesses. Primarily due to the work undertaken by Scottish Enterprise (and its predecessor the Scottish Development Agency), often assisted by the private sector, there has been a high level of experimentation in funding vehicles. Certainly the number and variety of schemes seems much larger than in any other UK region.

It is also evident that the funds, even the smaller funds, are not fully invested, suggesting that the deal flow has been insufficient, or that it has not been of a high quality. An equity gap may still exist and private sector funders are willing to recognise that this may be so. However, the involvement of public funding and the development of the private venture capital business have meant that, in Scotland, the risk/reward ratio and the size of funding package which can be accommodated has shifted. As a result, any funding gap is less important than it was historically and less than in other areas of the UK. Again, for early stage high growth companies there has been a significant development of debt/equity packages involving a mix of business angels, venture capital funding and SFLGS/bank lending.

The informal venture capital provided by business angels has become more important and more organised. Even in the early 1990s it was estimated by Scottish Enterprise that there were 1500 active business angels in Scotland investing some £13-25 million per annum. Of this, 75 per cent was estimated for start-ups and early stage financing.

In Scotland, as in the UK as a whole, there is general agreement that the existence of a funding gap may be a particular problem for high-tech businesses, but less consensus on the cause. One view is that high-tech funding does involve greater risk; another that the problem is lack of relevant technical skills and experience in potential funders. The most widely held view appears to be that because of the extended period involved in moving from the initial idea to a product or service which can be commercially marketed, the funding requirements of high-tech businesses are particularly large. Moreover, the timing and value of any income stream particularly uncertain. Further, for high-tech businesses, there does appear to be a greater reluctance on the part of the owner to part with equity. The equity 'panic button' appears to be a phenomenon as prevalent amongst business owners, as amongst the providers of venture capital.

Loan Finance

As far as the venture capital market is

concerned, the institutional structure of the business is very similar in Scotland to the remainder of GB. The same cannot be said about the provision of bank loans to new ventures and SMEs, the predominant form of external funding for these businesses. The three Scottish clearers - the Royal Bank of Scotland (RBS), the Bank of Scotland (BoS) and the Clydesdale Bank (CB) - dominate the market and the degree of dominance is greater than that evident in the rest of the UK, or for other bank services. This may raise competition issues, which we examine in section three. Here, we concentrate on whether there are any significant differences in the relationship between new ventures and SMEs in Scotland as compared with RUK.

For small value business lending, it is often difficult to distinguish between personal and business lending. Indeed, for new business ventures with no track record, any lending decision is likely to include a review of the personal financial record of the business owner; and

any lending is most likely to be secured against the owner's residential property. Again, an increasing number of small businesses are now obtaining business credit under the guise of personal borrowing, and that this can often be obtained from sources other than their main bank. For example, personal loans, credit cards and asset finance at point of sale are often used for business purposes.

The characteristics of lending to small businesses in Scotland do not appear to be significantly different from those reported for such lending in the UK as a whole. In a 1999 report the Bank of England suggested that, in the UK, there has been a movement away from overdraft funding toward a greater degree of term loan funding. Confidential data supplied to the author demonstrates a similar trend in Scotland. Again, for sole traders and small partnerships in particular, the ability to access more sources of personal finance often improved the supply of credit for business development purposes, as personal and business considerations were so closely interrelated.

Other Evidence

The remaining evidence relates mainly to the reported attitudes of business customers to their banks, which have reported in various surveys. All these surveys show a significant minority of customers who are critical of the level of service provided, but this is hardly exceptional in consumer surveys. What is of greater interest, from our present viewpoint, is how the Scottish banks emerge relative to the English banks in terms of their service to business customers, particularly new starts and SMEs.

The most detailed evidence is the surveys carried out for the Forum of Private Business in 1990, 1992, 1994, 1996, 1998 and 2000. Reviewing the 1990-98 surveys the DTI et al commented:

"There is evidence that there are regional differences between Scottish and English banks and their relationships with small business customers. Smaller banks may have a closer relationship with their small business customer (as in Scotland) and this may explain the continued finding of the FPB surveys that the smaller banks get higher ratings than the larger banks."[12]

On the basis of the same evidence Banks, Ennew and Reed concluded:

"The case of the Scottish banks, as perceived by their customers, was significantly different (to those of customers of English banks). There appeared to be less reliance on collateral for security purposes, loans tended to be shorter term and the general perception of banks by their customers were better".[13]

The 2000 survey is much less comforting in that Clydesdale Bank and the Bank of Scotland are given lower performance ratings than any of the 11 UK banks for which comparative information is available. Nonetheless, over the long period covered the Scottish banks

[12]*SME Research Database 1997*, Department of Trade and Industry et al. [13]*Private Business and Their Banks* (A report for the Forum of private Business) Banks and Ennew 1996

still outperform other clearers on the basis of customer satisfaction.

A comparative study of how banks approached risk assessment, found that when approached with a standard proposition:

"Scottish bank managers treated the proposition more favourably with 68% of Scottish bank managers prepared to fund the decision compared to the 50% split of the English management." [14]

This study concluded that Scottish banks put greater weight on non-financial aspects of lending, particularly the managerial skills and background of the entrepreneurs. Fletcher attributed this to the closer relationship between the bank manager and small business owner in Scotland (itself, presumably, a function of bank size).

The other survey evidence of interest has been carried through by MORI for Scottish Enterprise. The first survey (1992) found that the main problem people encountered when thinking of starting a business was business finance. This response was extraordinarily uniform in Scotland, England and Wales, Germany and the United States (the latter two economies are sometimes held up as offering particularly favourable institutional arrangements for SMEs).

This survey was repeated for Scotland in 1995, 1997 and 1999 and the results show a very substantial reduction in the percentage in Scotland who perceived finance to be the main problem. The other interesting finding from the surveys is that most of those who state that they are interested in starting a business haven't tried to do so i.e. they are not very serious 'wannabe' entrepreneurs. The great majority who did consult other parties about starting a business, report an encouraging response from the banks they approached – 70 per cent report that the bank was encouraging, only 10 per cent found the bank discouraging. As one Scottish Enterprise executive put it, "there is no evidence of the banks causing the (low birth rate) problem".

[14] 17th ISBA National Small Firms Policy and Research Conference 1994, Fletcher in DTI et al

3: Policy implications

While business density has increased in Scotland, there remains an entrepreneurial deficit relative to the GB as a whole. Much of this is due to the influence of London and the South East. The latter area has an exceptionally high business rate and a high business density and the gap between those two indicators in Scotland and the LSE has increased over time. Hence, the most substantial differences are not between Scotland and the rest of GB (excluding London and the rest of the South East) but between LSE and the rest of GB (including Scotland). In seeking solutions to the entrepreneurial deficit in Scotland, this finding should not be overlooked.

Two other general conclusions flow from this analysis. First, GB has long been a unified economy with a highly developed financial sector. Within such an economy, capital moves easily to areas/projects with higher returns. In short, there is no reason to suppose that new business starts and small and medium sized establishments (SMEs) should have any particular difficulty in obtaining access to loan or equity finance, compared with businesses in other areas of GB, provided they are as well managed. Of course, as in any market, imperfections exist. But the imperfections would have to be huge if they were the main factor behind the relatively low business density in Scotland and the increased entrepreneurial gap between Scotland and LSE over 1981-99.

Second, It is difficult to reconcile the very different business densities between rural and urban Scotland with the notion that imperfections in the provision of loan and equity capital are a major driver of any entrepreneurial deficit. As regards loan finance provided by banks, Scotland is the home of the development of joint stock, branch banking system, one of whose objectives was to funnel savings to areas/projects requiring financial support. It seems inherently implausible, therefore, that the Central Belt of Scotland, which, relative to much of rural Scotland has higher incomes and a more developed infrastructure, has a lower business density due to greater difficulties in accessing loan and equity funding.

Nonetheless, we still have to consider whether there is any objective contrary evidence that the entrepreneurial deficit in Scotland is due to the existence of financial constraints which have been peculiar to Scottish businesses. This is more usefully examined by considering whether there are any particular features of the supply of business funding in Scotland which might inhibit business development relative to the remainder of GB. As in the previous analysis, it is appropriate to distinguish between equity and debt funding.

Equity

A series of reports, and stated concerns over many years, suggest that there may be an equity gap in that high growth SMEs find it difficult to raise capital on acceptable terms. The scale of the problem is much more difficult to define, but it appears generally accepted that businesses may find it difficult to attract external equity funding for sums of less than £250,000, or possibly, over a much higher range of up to, say, £1 million.

However, there is also a widespread view that often the difficulty arises because the business owners are unprepared to accept any element of external control in the business. This may be a particular problem for high tech businesses. The issue does not appear to be that such investment is necessarily more risky than other business ventures, but rather that high tech businesses have a particular cash flow problem, in that there is often a long period between the development of the initial idea and its translation into a commercial product or service. These businesses require early capital funding and the funding required is often long-term and substantial. In these circumstances it is often difficult to persuade the owners of the business to surrender equity in the early life cycle of the business when venture capital funding is required.

There is no evidence that Scottish businesses suffer particularly from an equity gap. On the contrary, the private venture capital business appears to be particularly active in Scotland. Moreover, there is an emphasis on early funding and business expansion funding of smaller average size than GB as a whole, which would imply that any equity gap is likely to be less important in Scotland.

There is also is a long history of public sector assisted funds whose raison d'être has been to address any equity gap. The average investment of these funds is usually below £200,000 and always below £300,000, the range in which the equity gap is usually expected to operate. Further, although those funds are generally small, none appear to have exhausted the fund established; that is, all the funds could find equity and/or loan capital if there were more good business ventures seeking finance.

If there is a problem in Scotland arising from these initiatives, it seems likely to be that there are too many small public sector assisted funds. These will have high management/ administrative costs and will find it extremely difficult to attract and retain good quality professional staff. There is a clear case here for a review of the effectiveness of existing arrangements. In all likelihood, the optimal outcome would be fewer, larger funds, with a higher degree of professional management.

We conclude that any entrepreneurial deficit in Scotland is not due to a particular problem with equity funding. On the contrary, there is an active formal venture capital sector in Scotland, a growing involvement of business angels and a very 'hands-on' approach by Scottish Enterprise, the LECs and the local authorities, usually assisted by ERDF funding. In this process, the Scottish banks have often been involved, both in establishing some of the recent funds and working with these other parties to provide appropriate funding packages.

Debt

The evidence on debt funding, in which the banks play the key role, is much softer, mainly because there is so little statistical information on the comparative practice of banks. However, as far as business attitudes are concerned, these appear to be more favourable towards the Scottish banks as a whole, than to their English counterparts.

Possibly more interesting in this regard is the survey evidence provided by Scottish Enterprise. This supports three key conclusions. First, on the only occasion on which the question was asked (in 1992) the majority of respondents in Scotland, England and Wales, Germany and the United States, all considered that the difficulty in accessing finance was the chief barrier to starting a business. Yet, the differences between the proportions reporting this as the main barrier were remarkably small, given the very different institutional arrangements and circumstances of these different economies. Second, the proportion of respondents considering that access to finance was the main problem fell sharply in Scotland over 1992-9. Third, as one moves from respondents who are simply 'wannabe' entrepreneurs to those who had taken some positive steps to establish a business, the proportion considering access to finance as the problem diminishes substantially.

The UK market for most retail banking products is fragmented and clearly contestable. This is most evident in the manner in which new entrants have been able to obtain significant market share for products, such as new mortgages and credit cards. A number of major financial institutions now compete directly with the traditional clearers and a wide range of retail banking products are also offered by non-banks. Telecommunications and information technology have lowered the cost of market entry and this is likely to be taken further by the internet.

While the market for most retail bank

products is contestable and is contested, small business lending in Scotland is dominated by the three Scottish clearers and their market share (in terms of main-lead bank) has not changed appreciably over a period of years. The degree of market concentration is higher than in England and Wales where the four main English clearers account for almost 84 per cent of the lending to small businesses (Bank of England, 1999). Yet, while the Scottish clearers do have a high share of the market for loans to SMEs, this has not been acquired at the expense of their business customers.

The Entrepreneurial Deficit

The puzzle remains, why is there an entrepreneurial deficit in the Central Belt and what should be done about it? There is no easy answer to this puzzle. For example, an unpublished study prepared for the Business Birth Rate Strategy demonstrated that the deficit was not a product of industrial structure. Across the main industrial sectors the Scottish birth rate is behind that of GB as a whole, and is particularly low relative to London and the South East.

An explanation, which has been given some credence, is that low home ownership in Scotland made it difficult for potential (or actual) entrepreneurs to provide sufficient security against bank borrowing. Hence, it might be argued, the lower birth rate and, consequently, the comparative absence of high growth businesses. Indeed, there is evidence that low business density, across the British regions, is correlated with low home ownership, and vice versa. It is much more doubtful if the observed correlation denotes cause and effect. Equally plausibly, the factors that are associated with low home ownership might also be associated with a low rate of business formation; in short, the correlation appears to reflect an aversion to risk which, historically, inhibited both home ownership and business formation.

Even if low home ownership was important historically, its relevance must be diminishing. In 1980, owner occupiers only accounted for 39 per cent of the housing stock in Scotland; this has now risen to 60 per cent, much closer to the GB average (67 per cent). Much of this is due to the 'right to buy' legislation and it may be that much of the resultant increase in personal equity still lies ahead of us. Even if we accepted this, however, it must be regarded as an issue of diminishing importance, already taken care of by relevant policy changes involved in the 'right to buy' legislation.

The really significant entrepreneurial deficit is not between Scotland and the rest of GB outside London and the South East, but between the latter area and the rest of GB. The reasons for this are complex but London and the South East appears to possess certain critical advantages which result in a high rate of business formation – for example, a large catchment area with an affluent population; a social climate which encourages individualisation and does not put much weight on collective action; an awareness of the rewards of entrepreneurial success and willingness to take risks to share in these rewards; the presence of technologically advanced businesses and business HQ functions; a high representation of small, problem solving businesses with a strong commitment to R&D and new product/ service developments; a thriving tradeable services sector; and a living environment which is attractive to new immigrants, an important source of new business development.

By way of contrast, the Central Belt of Scotland, like certain other older industrial areas (e.g. the North East, Merseyside and South Wales) does not provide an environment which is favourable to new business births. The reasons for this are certainly debatable. The economic history of these areas is likely to have been influential, particularly their previous dependence on the heavy industries. Again, in the long period of their decline, there was a marked reluctance to embrace the need for economic change, particularly the increasing importance of tradeable services. In Central Scotland particularly, the risk/reward ratio seems more biased toward public sector employment compared with private sector employment and social attitudes which value professional careers ahead of business careers.

Whatever the causes of the entrepreneurial deficit in Scotland, there is no evidence that it is due to inappropriate and unsupportive financial institutions. The problem appears to be on the 'demand' side, not the 'supply': that is, the attitudes and values of the resident population produce, particularly relative to London and the South East, fewer people who are prepared to take on the risks associated with establishing and growing in new business. As new business creation is extremely important in creating new employment opportunities, it is hardly surprising that Scottish employment and aggregate income growth have lagged behind the UK over many decades.

The prevailing pattern of population mobility will aggravate the underlying situation. Scots pride themselves on their capacity for inventiveness and hard work. Yet, many of our business icons have felt it necessary to leave Scotland to develop their talents. Migration is always a selective process and migration from Scotland has always tended to include a higher population of those with entrepreneurial ability. Equally, Scotland has never attracted the successive flows of immigrants of different national and ethnic origins which have been so important to London and the South East. Which is the chicken and which is the egg in this process is difficult to establish. But Scotland still appears excluded from the virtuous circle of a favourable business environment which attracts and retains able business people, thus enhancing a favourable business environment.

Scottish Enterprise, through its business birth rate strategy, is the only Scottish institution which has made any serious attempt to address this problem. It is fair to conclude (as with Dow and Kirk[15]) that there is, as yet, no evidence that this has had any discernible impact. Indeed, the problem is so deep-rooted that any

[15]See *The Numbers of Scottish Businesses and Economic Policy*, Dow & Kirk, Department of Economics and Enterprise Glasgow Caledonia University, published in The Fraser of Allander Institute Quarterly Economic Commentary October 2000

pay-back is bound to be over a long period. Moreover, it is unrealistic to expect any government agency to have much impact acting on its own. Inevitably, given the large numbers of small businesses, any intervention by Scottish Enterprise has to be selective. As has often been observed of government policy toward larger corporates, 'government policy starts with finding the winners and ends with the losers finding the government'. A selective policy of picking small businesses with growth potential is likely to encounter the same fate.

If the essential problem is on the demand side, then we require a significant favourable change in the risk-reward ratio as perceived by people who might consider establishing a new business (or growing a small business). Given that the behaviour pattern to be changed is entrenched, the signal must be powerful and real, not mere words and flummery. The new local enterprise forums will be a prime example of the latter!

Two complementary policies suggest themselves. First public expenditure is a higher proportion of national income in Scotland than in the UK as a whole. A corollary of this is that public sector employment is a higher proportion of total employment. This is a version of the "too few producers" problem experienced by the UK in the 1990s. Moreover, given the manner in which public sector salaries are negotiated, the gap between Scottish/GB incomes in the public sector is likely to be much narrower than that between Scottish/GB private sector earnings. In short the risk-reward ratio is tipped in favour of the public sector employment rather than private sector employment. I understand that the Policy Institute will be reviewing the relationship between public and private sector reward structure in a subsequent publication. If this confirms the analysis then there should be a general presumption against increasing public expenditure as a share of total Scottish income. This implies that the Scottish Parliament should not apply its discretionary power to raise the standard rate of income tax. This would clearly be the 'wrong' signal given Scottish circumstances.

Second, there is a pressing need to improve the financial incentives for new starts and small businesses. In this regard, the only general instrument available to the Scottish Parliament is the local business rate. Yet, it is well suited for the purpose, as property costs are an important element in the cost structure of most new and small businesses. Historically, Scotland's record in this area is quite dreadful. Left to themselves Scottish local authorities happily raised the business rates while holding down domestic rates. This was politically convenient but highly damaging for new starts and small businesses. For comparable businesses the business rate was much higher in Scotland than in the rest of GB. The higher cost base was either passed on to consumers thus depressing sales, or else assisted in lower margins thus depressing profits and discouraging new starts.

In the 1980s and 1990s the movement toward a uniform business rate reduced but did not remove the Scottish anomaly and the clear and present danger is a reversion to type and a rise in local business rates in Scotland. What is required is the reverse movement - a large and sustained reduction in local business rates as a clear and unmistakable statement of intent. For a determined administration with a clear sense of the important economic priorities, an abolition of the local business rate would be a quite feasible financial target.

Over many generations the Scottish political elite has proved remarkably resistant to the notion that the establishment and growth of small businesses is a necessary requirement of a successful economy. Even where the elite speaks the right words there is a strong suspicion that they do not understand the meaning of the language; or, at least, that the words do not result in any meaningful action. Yet the low business birth rate remains the Achilles heel of the Scottish economy. Until it is rectified do not expect any sustained improvement in our rate of economic development.

A Tax Whose Time has Passed

Jim and Margaret Cuthbert

A looming Catch-22 on business rates threatens to result in a higher burden on business profits in Scotland, with adverse effects on enterprise, new business formation and growth. The best solution would be to abolish non-domestic rates at UK level. The small loss of fiscal autonomy for the Scottish Executive would be a price worth paying.

The topic of non-domestic rates is of considerable concern to business, particularly small businesses. But it hardly features in the consciousness of the public. But it should be at the centre of Scottish political debate. The system of non-domestic rates is likely to have a significantly adverse effect on enterprise in Scotland and is also likely, in due course, to lead to a disproportionate squeeze on public expenditure as a whole in Scotland, compared to England.

Historically, there had been justified concern in the business community in Scotland that the impact of non-domestic rates represented a differential cost penalty on Scottish businesses compared with those in England. The clas-

sic, if possibly apocryphal, example, was that Lewis's in Argyll Street in Glasgow paid more in non-domestic rates than Selfridge's in London.

In the early 1990s, the then Conservative government introduced its solution: that of the unified business rate. Through the early 1990s, the average non-domestic rate per £ (that is, the rate poundage) was progressively reduced in Scotland, until in 1995/96, parity was achieved with England at a rate of 43.2p in the £. At the same time, the Treasury made substantial payments into the Scottish Block, to compensate for the loss of revenue that would otherwise have been experienced.

At the time of devolution, therefore,

there were two key features of the non-domestic rates system. First, there was a unified business rate throughout Scotland and England. Second, non-domestic rate income was part of the Scottish Block, in the sense that it was one of the sources of finance that was paid into the Scottish Block. Since changes in the aggregate Block were determined by the Barnett formula alone, this meant that public expenditure in Scotland was insulated from changes in non-domestic rates income in Scotland. To all intents and purposes, non-domestic rates could be regarded as simply another UK tax, like income tax, paid into the central exchequer, but with the oddity that local authorities played a role in collecting the tax.

Devolution swept away these key features, although the profound implications of the changes were perhaps not immediately apparent. Non-domestic rates are a devolved issue, which means that the Scottish Executive has the power to set the business rate in Scotland (and, indeed, to make more

fundamental changes, like setting a differential local business rate). But there would have been no point in allowing the Scottish Executive to set the rate poundage, if non-domestic rate income stayed within the Departmental Expenditure Limit, (or DEL, as it is commonly known), since changes to the DEL are entirely determined by the Barnett formula. (The DEL is the post-devolution equivalent of the Scottish Block.) So another change which took place with devolution was that non-domestic rates moved out of the Block/DEL, to become a separate source of revenue for the Scottish Executive. If more revenue is collected through non-domestic rates in Scotland, public expenditure in Scotland can rise, and vice-versa. Correspondingly, changes in non-domestic rate income in England do not generate Barnett formula consequences for Scotland.[1]

These changes to the treatment of non-domestic rates relative to the DEL are, from one point of view, entirely logical. There is no point in giving the

[1] Source: HM Treasury, *Funding the Scottish Parliament*, 31 March, 1999

Scottish Executive the power to change the rate poundage in Scotland, if it cannot benefit from any extra revenue so raised. But there is one large fly in this particular ointment. The revenue raised by non-domestic rates depends not only on the rate poundage, but also on the size of the tax base, which is determined by the number of premises subject to non-domestic rates, and on the average rateable value for these premises.

The problem is that neither of these two factors is within the control of the Scottish Executive. The implications could be very serious. Suppose, for example, that the underlying trend in the number of premises, or the average rateable value for these premises, was increasing faster in England than in Scotland. This would mean that, with the same poundage in Scotland and England, the total revenue from non-domestic rates in England would rise faster than in Scotland.

This higher level of non-domestic rate income in England could be used in one of two ways. It could be spent, so raising overall levels of public expenditure in England. But since public expenditure in England funded from non-domestic rates does not feed into the Barnett formula, Scotland would receive no increase in its DEL. So public expenditure in England would rise, while public expenditure in Scotland would stay the same. Alternatively, the higher non-domestic rates income in England could be used to displace other forms of funding. For example, central government grants to local authorities could be reduced, since English authorities were now receiving more non-domestic rates income. In this case, public expenditure in England would not increase. But, since grant payments to local authorities in England do feed into the Barnett formula, the Scottish DEL would be reduced by the Barnett formula consequence of the reduction in the English grant payments. In this case, therefore, Scottish public expenditure would be squeezed downward.

Either way, moving non-domestic rates out of the DEL means that public expenditure in Scotland will be squeezed relative to England, if the underlying growth in the non-domestic rates tax base is higher in England than in Scotland, unless the rate poundage in Scotland increases relative to that in England in order to compensate.

How significant could such a squeeze be? Currently, non-domestic rates contribute over £1.5 billion to the funding of the Scottish Executive.[2] If non-domestic rate revenues in England rose by 10 per cent more than those in Scotland, and the extra revenue was used to displace the payment of grant to local authorities in England, then Scotland would experience, through the Barnett formula, a reduction to its DEL equivalent to about 10 per cent of non-domestic rate revenues in Scotland. This would represent a reduction of about £150 million, equivalent to about 1 per cent of the current total Scottish DEL. The amounts involved in a potential non-domestic rates squeeze are therefore significant, relative to the funding resources of the Scottish Executive.

The rateable value of business premises is, in theory, related to the notional rental value of the property. In order to reflect changes in average rent levels for different types of property and in different areas, revaluations of the non-domestic rate base are carried out every five years. The most recent revaluation took effect in April 2000 in both England and Scotland. Before the revaluation, the unified business rate poundage in both England and Scotland was 48.9 pence in the £. When the government announced the provisional rate poundage figures that would apply after the revaluation, it was estimated that the effect of the revaluation would be to increase the tax base by around 24 per cent in England, as compared to 12 per cent in Scotland.[3] The latest estimate now puts the revaluation factor in Scotland at 15 per cent.[4] At face value, these figures do indeed seem to give clear-cut evidence that the tax base is indeed rising faster in England than in Scotland.

The government adopted the princi-

[2]Source: Scottish Executive, *Investing in You*.
[3]Source: Scottish Executive Press release, *SE0136/2000*.
[4]Source: Scottish Executive, December 2000.

ple that the aim of the revaluation in Scotland, (and similarly in England), was to raise the same amount in tax in real terms as before the revaluation. As the Scottish base had not gone up by as much as the English base, henceforth the Scottish rate poundage would have to be higher than that in England. Accordingly, in December 1999, Jack McConnell announced a provisional rate poundage in Scotland of 45.8 pence in the £ for 2000/01: whereas the provisional figure for England was set at 41.6 pence. In other words, the Scottish business rate poundage, from parity with England in 1999/2000, rose to some 10 per cent higher than England in 2000/2001.

What effect is this likely to have on the relative competitiveness of businesses? One argument that could be advanced is that the key factor in determining the burden of non-domestic rates is the actual amount of money paid over in the form of rates. On this argument, while the average business in England has experienced a larger increase in rate-able value (but is faced with a correspondingly lower rate poundage) than the average business in Scotland, there has, however, been no change in relative burden since the amount which both average businesses are paying out in rates is unchanged. This, presumably, would be the government's position (since if they do not adopt a position like this, it amounts to admitting that the recent revaluation has involved a change in relative burden). However, this argument is disingenuous.

A strong case can be made for saying that an equitable way to assess the burden of non-domestic rates is to consider the amount of non-domestic rates paid per unit of profit. The critical question, therefore, is whether the larger increase in rateable values in England, which corresponds to higher nominal rental values in England, indicates a greater ability to generate profits from the business premises in question. Overall, it seems clear that a substantial element of the increase in rental values in England will indeed correspond to a greater potential to generate profits. This is particularly so given the booming state of the economy in much of southern England. On this view, levying the same money amount in non-domestic rates from the average business in England will represent a reduced rates burden in England per unit of profit compared with Scotland.

If future revaluations follow the same pattern, the implication is that Scottish businesses can anticipate an increasingly severe differential business rate penalty relative to England. This will have an adverse effect on enterprise and new business creation in Scotland. To avoid this happening, the only route for the Scottish Executive is to abstain from increasing the Scottish rate poundage relative to England at each revaluation. But if the Scottish Executive chooses this option, it will then have to live with the consequences of the squeeze on public expenditure in Scotland implied by the relatively lower growth of non-domestic rate revenue.

In effect, government finds itself in a Catch 22. If it takes the view that a uni-fied business rate should be maintained between Scotland and England, then the higher average revaluation factor in England means that non-domestic rate revenue in England will increase faster than that in Scotland. This, given the way the devolution package has been set up, implies a significant relative squeeze on public expenditure in Scotland. Conversely, if government opts (as it has done) for a higher rate poundage in Scotland, it will avoid the immediate public expenditure trap, but at the penalty of imposing a relatively higher burden on business profits in Scotland, with consequent adverse effects on enterprise, new business formation, and future GDP growth. Moreover, the public expenditure trap will still re-open under another guise, since the cost penalty on Scottish business will lead to a lower growth rate in the number of firms in Scotland. This has the same end effect of a lower relative growth in the tax base. Overall, neither of the options open to government appears either attractive or sustainable.

This paper has been concerned with an aspect of non-domestic rates of particular concern in Scotland, namely, the interaction between the non-domestic rates system and the devolution settlement. We have not gone into the other well established adverse effects of non-domestic rates, particularly the disproportionately heavy burden it places on small businesses. Figures from the Federation of Small Businesses indicate that non-domestic rates represent on average over 13 per cent of overheads for small businesses, compared with about 3 per cent for large businesses.[5] This disproportionate effect will tend to inhibit new business creation. Nor have we considered the differential effect of non-domestic rates on different business sectors. If a business works from domestic premises, it will avoid non-domestic rates. Indeed, many businesses do function from domestic properties. There will, however, be a strong sectoral effect, since small businesses in the service sector can much more readily operate from domestic premises than those in manufacturing.

This could have a profound effect in the long run on the sectoral distribution of indigenous business. Indeed, it is likely that the historic high non-domestic rates burden in Scotland has played a part in contributing to Scotland's current acknowledged weakness in indigenous manufacturing companies.

Because of the way that non-domestic rates have been handled in the funding arrangements for devolution, Scotland can anticipate that the Scottish non-domestic rates poundage will continue to rise in future relative to that in England, with consequent adverse effects on enterprise and business creation, and with the danger of a vicious circle becoming established, where the higher rate poundage further reduces the growth in the tax base in Scotland, making the original problem worse. At the same time, public expenditure in Scotland is likely to be squeezed, if the Scottish Executive attempts to tackle the problem by restricting the growth in Scotland's rate poundage.

What is the solution? Within the

[5]Federation of Small Businesses: written evidence to the Local Government Committee of the Scottish Parliament: 8th Report, 2000

framework of the existing devolution settlement, it appears that there is little scope to tackle the problem. Looking more broadly, the most satisfactory solution could well be to take the radical step of abolishing non-domestic rates altogether. This is a decision that would have to be taken at UK level, and would have to be accompanied by a corresponding increase in some other form of business taxation - probably corporation tax. For Scotland, the advantages of escaping from the non-domestic rates trap would be offset by the loss of what amounts to a degree of fiscal autonomy currently enjoyed by the Scottish Executive. However, the disadvantages of this particular element of fiscal autonomy almost certainly far outweigh any advantages.

There is, in fact, a general lesson to be drawn from this particular example, which is relevant to the wider debate about whether the Scottish Executive should seek or be granted more fiscal autonomy in other areas. The limited degree of fiscal autonomy involved in the current non-domestic rates arrangements could only be made to work if the non-domestic rates tax base in Scotland grows at least as fast as that in England. However, the Scottish Executive does not have the economic powers to put in place policies to make it likely that the tax base would enjoy this degree of growth. Without these powers, (and they would have to be wide ranging powers indeed), the limited fiscal autonomy the Scottish Executive has in respect of non-domestic rates simply amounts to a millstone. The moral is clear: fiscal autonomy for the Scottish Executive is likely to be counter-productive unless accompanied by very significant economic powers.

The general lesson we would draw is that any proposals for further fiscal autonomy for the Scottish Executive should be considered with very great care: and unless such proposals are accompanied by the granting to the Scottish Executive of appropriate and sufficient economic powers, such proposals should probably be rejected.

As presently constituted, the present arrangements for non domestic rates represent a measure of fiscal autonomy for the Scottish Executive which will probably be unworkable, given the Scottish Executive's lack of powers to put in place policies to ensure that the non domestic rates base grows quickly enough. The granting of sufficient powers to the Scottish Executive to make the non domestic rates system workable does not appear, in current circumstances, to be either a feasible or a realistic prospect. We argue, therefore, that, particularly given the other general disadvantages of the non domestic rates system, the way out is to abolish non-domestic rates at UK level, replacing it probably by an increase in Corporation Tax. The resultant small loss of fiscal autonomy for the Scottish Executive would be a price worth paying.

Scotland's falling rate of business start-ups

During the first six months of 2000, a total of 8,855 new businesses were created in Scotland. This represents a reduction of 16 per cent compared with the same period in 1999, and a continuation of the trend seen in 1999, where business starts also fell by 16 per cent over a six month period.

The third quarter data shows a slight levelling off in the rate of start-up decline. The number of businesses started in the third quarter of 2000 was 4,252, down 3.6 per cent on the same quarter of 1999. The cumulative data for the first nine months of 2000 shows 13,107 businesses were started in the first nine months, a 12.4 per cent reduction on the first three quarters of 1999.Business rates place an unfair burden on small firms which can find themselves paying five times as much as large firms as a percentage of profits. Relief should be targeted, not on the location of the business or size of premises, but on the profits of the business itself and its ability to pay. Threshholds should be avoided and relief delivered on a taper.

Rates reform: size matters

Gerry Dowds

Business rates place an unfair burden on small firms which can find themselves paying five times as much as large firms as a percentage of profits. Relief should be targeted, not on the location of the business or size of premises, but on the profits of the business itself and its ability to pay. Threshholds should be avoided and relief delivered on a taper.

When the old Scottish Parliament packed its bags and moved to Westminster in 1707, it was said the baggage contained a property tax based on property valuation: the precursor of the present valuation and rating system. If this tale is true, then it is appropriate that the new Scottish Parliament is considering how to make major changes to business rating to ease the burden on smaller businesses.

Business rates is payable on all non-domestic properties and that even includes public conveniences and cemeteries, run by local authorities. Consecutive Governments have valued business rates as an easy-to-collect means of at least partially funding Local Government.

Until 1985, valuation and rating applied to domestic as well as non-domestic property. In that year, revaluation hit Scotland with some force. The quinquennial revaluation should have been applied two years earlier but had been postponed. England and Wales had waited even longer - thirteen years - and would have to wait another five years. The results of heavy campaigning by both domestic and commercial ratepayers were the poll tax and the Uniform Business Rate (UBR).

Scottish businesses welcomed UBR as it meant that business rate poundage would be levelled out at an average for all of Scotland and England, with control of rate poundage taken away from local authorities. Another, more immediate result, initially for Scotland was 'revaluation rate relief' and then after 1990, for all of the UK, was Transitional Relief and that is with us today. Transitional relief has made a relatively simple tax complex but it is an essential help to small firms until a more permanent relief scheme can be put in place.

Research by the Department of the Environment in 1995 showed that business rate places an inequitable burden on smaller firms- with small firms paying five times proportionately more than large firms as a percentage of gross profits. At the end of 1999, then Finance Minister, Jack McConnell, agreed that a Small Business Rates Relief Scheme was required to ease that burden.

A small business rates relief scheme is needed as-

● Smaller businesses pay much higher proportions of both turnover and profit in rates than larger businesses.

● Smaller businesses are subject to much higher rates per square foot than larger businesses.

● Occupancy represents a far higher proportion of the costs for small businesses than for large ones, so a tax based on rental value is bound to bear disproportionately.

Concern about the impact of business rates on business has been the highest priority issue in every quarterly survey of FPB members' opinions since the 1st quarter of 1997 and the issue has featured in the top three for the past 15 years. In spring 1999, FPB Scotland conducted a major pre-election survey of members' attitudes that included the key question:

"The new Scottish Parliament will have the power to legislate on a number of important issues that could affect your business. Which issues are you aware of and which are important to your business?"

The results showed that small businesses regarded the first priority for the Scottish Parliament was to take urgent action on business rates and introduce a simple, effective and long-term small business relief scheme.

FPB Scotland proposes that the criteria to be used in determining the eligibility of rates relief should incorporate the following principles:

● **Relief should be targeted at size of business irrespective of location.**
The smaller the business, the greater the relief - this is because of the close relationship between size and the impact of rates as shown by Government statistics

● **Size should be measured on current information.**
(Preferably already subject to collection) which reflects the businesses current circumstances and which is robust and reliable.

● **Relief should be aimed at businesses rather than premises.**
This is firstly because large businesses occupy small premises (and vice versa) and secondly because relief targeted at the property will be capitalised into the rental value and be reflected in an increase in the rent, ensuring that the ultimate beneficiary will be the landlord not the occupier.

● **Relief should be delivered through an alternative mechanism to that of rates.** This would ensure the separation of the relief from the property market and hence the risk that it might pose would lie with the property owner rather than the small business.

● **A platform for long term stability should be provided rather than a temporary fix.**

● **Thresholds should be avoided.**
This is because of the impact on incentive to expand, and unfair competition between businesses around the margin - i.e. relief should be delivered on a taper.

● **The system should be simple for business and public authorities to apply and administer.**

● **Disruption to the current system should be minimised.**

● **Relief should be funded either by shifting the burden, broadening the current rate base or from central funds.**

The most popular criterion among

FPB members as the base for relief is the previous year's profits, as this supports the "Ability to Pay" principle. While FPB Scotland would be content with this, for technical reasons it recommends that it be based on employers' National Insurance liability, a good proxy for employment. An FPB Referendum of members' views in October 1996 found that 84 per cent of members believed that it would be fairer to use National Insurance liability rather than property values to underpin rates relief. And in May 1998, almost 90 per cent of members rejected using rateable value as the measure of "smallness".

National Insurance (NI) liability has the following advantages:

* The figure is readily available and is easily checked by both business and Government

* It is less volatile than profit or turnover

* The information is more up-to-date than Rateable Values

* Levels of NI are determined by employment numbers and salary levels thus providing a fair measure of size and resources

* The figure is not subject to complications caused by changes in value following an appeal that may bring a business below the threshold

* It enables delivery of a tapered relief to avoid the competitive distortions created by thresholds

* Relief could be delivered centrally through the PAYE system

In November 1999, FPB Scotland's rates relief proposals were presented to the Scottish Parliament's Local Government Committee and gained their approval. It argued for a 'tapered' scheme saying that a scheme based on a rateable valuation threshold would be unfair to firms operating around the threshold.

They said *'that consideration should be given to the use of some other means - for example, national insurance contributions (as suggested by the Forum of Private Business in Scotland) or business turnover - in order to identify genuinely small businesses...'*

It is sometimes argued that using employment levels as a base might discourage growth. FPB Scotland responds that firstly any system based on size must face the same criticisms and is unavoidable if relief is to be focused on small businesses. In addition a tapered system such as FPB Scotland proposes means that its effect would be negligible, as it will not be the determining criteria at any one point.

Indeed, far from providing a disincentive to employment growth, the direct impact of the scheme will be to significantly reduce the incidence of tax on smaller employers, by shifting the burden to larger employers. As such the scheme will significantly (given the impact of rates on smaller businesses) add to the financial resource and hence propensity to expand of those businesses.

The correct comparison is with the alternative of no relief, or a relief which does not focus on the size of the business. It must be self evident that either of these scenarios is less encouraging of employment creation by smaller businesses.

Business rates are the principal tax faced by small businesses and increases cause a competitive disadvantage. The FPB has stressed that UBR starts at a far higher level from the first pound than the other major taxes (Corporation Tax, Income Tax, National Insurance, VAT) and lobbies for this to be addressed.

Since devolution, Scotland is in the unique position of setting the pace in the UK and adoption of an effective small business rates relief would show that the Executive supports small businesses in playing their part in the future prosperity of Scotland.

Oh, no, not Friday afternoon

Alastair Balfour

A high business birth and survival rate critically depends on a supportive culture for entrepreneurs. But the growing regulatory burden on business, imposed with scant regard to cost, threatens both the viability of small firms and the aspiration to launch new ones. SMEs are now at the point of 'significant rebellion' unless urgent steps are taken to halt the job-killing bureaucratic onslaught.

It's Friday afternoon. Wash-up time in many SMEs, when the many outstanding issues after another frantic week are put to bed by the more organised managements, to allow a fresh start on Monday.

For the sales team, it's going back through the paperwork to make sure the bookings, credit checks and other processes are done. For the production people it's sitting down to assess why output was below target again, and finalising an action plan to tackle the blockages in the system.

For personnel, there's a review of progress on the Investors in People paperwork and finalising the jobs advert to go into the papers next week. For accounts, it's reconciling cash with bank statements and preparing another round of payment cheques for directors' signatures.

And so on, through each part of the business. Essential internal maintenance, to keep the machinery running as smoothly as possible and keep the inescapable paper mountain from toppling over and burying everyone beneath a pile of bumph.

But in all of this catch-up activity there's one person in the business who, somehow, never seems to catch up on the piles in their in-tray. It's usually the company secretary who, in a small owner-managed organisation, is often the finance director, maybe too the systems manager and perhaps a couple of other jobs as well. As principal keeper of the faith, responsible for ensuring that the business complies with its statutory obligations, this is the person who is the front line of business's eternal war against stifling government regulation.

Ask any SME managing director, indeed ask any SME company secretary if you can persuade them to lift their heads from paperwork, and you will find that they are heartily sick of form filling and regulation. Every month, it seems, another closely-spaced document appears from another government department requiring completion and compliance - and requiring it in a way that makes plain the penalties if the job is not done.

Now, the rising tide of protests from business lobby groups about this rising tide of forms may leave the impression in the minds of the public that compa-nies can't be bothered with providing the essential data that the government machine requires to plan its strategy. Not so.

While their inflexibility irks some times, business accepts that departments like the Inland Revenue (PAYE) and HM Customs and Excise (VAT) are absolutely due their paperwork and cheques on time. The government needs funded, and it's business and their employees who do it. Fair enough.

It's also largely fair enough to expect that departments like Employment and Trade & Industry need regular statistical information so they can monitor the economy.

But what is currently causing a new outbreak of protest about red tape is the latest raft of regulation to hit business's in-tray as New Labour enthusiastically implements the social changes promised in its manifesto and the new Brussels outbreak of human rights legislation. In the past two years it's been the massive Working Time Regulations, reckoned to add £7bn to business's costs UK-wide, coupled with the National Minimum Wage (a mere £4.5bn) that have caused the most hassle. By comparison the latest Working Families Tax Credit (£220m) scheme is a breeze.

Bad enough, but now looms the introduction of Stakeholder Pensions, Parental Leave, EU Directives on Waste Water, controls on Teleworking and other exciting initiatives badly needed to prevent over-exploitation of people and the environment by ruthless companies.

Ask SME directors what they privately feel about this wave of regulation, and a majority (although probably not a huge majority) will frankly admit to being in two minds over it. Personally, they usually agree with the principle behind most of the new laws. After all they are human beings and well appreciate the need for improvement in the general quality of life at a time when the benefits of business success are certainly not being spread evenly across society.

Professionally, they are at a loss to understand how they are expected to comply with them without suffering increased costs, reduced competitiveness and lower profits - the classic formula that generally produces reduced employment.

In business's view, it is this consistent failure on the part of ministers and civil servants to appreciate the direct linkage between additional regulation, higher costs and fewer jobs that most dismays directors. In the past it was usually possible to find ways of absorbing extra administration costs. Today, bluntly, it isn't.

Remember, in the hurly-burly of business in an ever-more competitive climate, SMEs have no spare administration resources to throw at the paperwork problem. Indeed they often have less. 'Admin' is increasingly seen as an unwarranted overhead cost on efficiency-driven organisations. Companies have been cutting those costs, paring their financial and secretarial functions to concentrate resources on the key areas of product development, technology investment and selling. Which means the bumph buck stops firmly with that over-pressed company secretary.

One thing is now for sure: business has absolutely no faith in government's ability to rein in the bureaucrats. Initiative after initiative has failed to reduce the regulatory burden. The civil service mentality is to regulate and complicate and ministers appear helpless to change that culture.

SMEs well understand that they are expected to provide the continual growth in employment which government needs. Now, it seems they are at the point of significant rebellion against regulation which could well threaten that objective. Because while some businesses and markets have little alternative but to fuel growth with people, increasingly others have the option of using systems and software to automate their processes. It's always been the prime cost-reduction weapon, reducing head-count through investment in machinery.

Now, I suspect, we are about to see a further twist to that particular screw. Because business people are above all pragmatists - they have to be to survive. They may (and will) shout and campaign about over-regulation. But ultimately they know full well this government is unlikely to back off from its drive to reform society for the better. So at the same time as they campaign, they will quietly get on with the essential task of taking cost out of their operations: in other words, people.

T'was always thus.

Forthcoming publications

**A series of major papers are planned for the first half of 2001.
The Institute attaches high importance to thorough academic research, clarity
of expression and fresh and innovative proposals that can be carried forward
for policy.**

Spring 2001 publications include:

Professor Sir Alan Peacock and others on *Who Pays the Piper?* – a critique of
public arts funding in Scotland and proposals for reform

Professor James Tooley on the state of public education in Scotland

George Kerevan and others on a critique of the economy in Scotland and new
policies and proposals to lift growth and performance

Other topics under preparation include healthcare in Scotland; Scotland and the
euro; a critique of agriculture policy in Scotland and proposals for reform;
a graphic primer on economics; and an Adam Smith primer for students.

Policy Institute publications are targeted at key policymakers and opinion formers
in Scotland; leading businesses and financial institutions throughout Scotland and
business organisations and lobby groups; members of the Scottish parliament and
Executive; schools and universities and key commentators in the media.

If you are interested in writing for or contributing to the work of the Institute, or
sponsoring a publication and programme of events and seminars, please write to:
**The Director, The Policy Institute, Barclay House, 108 Holyrood Road,
Edinburgh EH8 8AS.**